Cooperative Learning:
Increasing College Faculty Instructional Productivity

by David W. Johnson, Roger T. Johnson, and Karl A. Smith

ASHE-ERIC Higher Education Report No. 4, 1991

Prepared by

Clearinghouse on Higher Education
The George Washington University

In cooperation with

ASHE

Association for the Study
Of Higher Education

Published by

School of Education and Human Development
The George Washington University

Jonathan D. Fife, Series Editor

Cite as
Johnson, David W., Roger T. Johnson, and Karl A. Smith. 1991.
*Cooperative Learning: Increasing College Faculty Instructional
Productivity.* ASHE-ERIC Higher Education Report No. 4.
Washington, D.C.: The George Washington University, School
of Education and Human Development.

Library of Congress Catalog Card Number 91-066915
ISSN 0884-0040
ISBN 1-878380-09-5

Managing Editor: Bryan Hollister
Manuscript Editor: Barbara Fishel, Editech
Cover design by Michael David Brown, Rockville, Maryland

The ERIC Clearinghouse on Higher Education invites individuals to submit proposals for writing monographs for the
ASHE-ERIC Higher Education Report series. Proposals must
include:
1. A detailed manuscript proposal of not more than five pages.
2. A chapter-by-chapter outline.
3. A 75-word summary to be used by several review commit-
   tees for the initial screening and rating of each proposal.
4. A vita and a writing sample.

ERIC **Clearinghouse on Higher Education**
School of Education and Human Development
The George Washington University
One Dupont Circle, Suite 630
Washington, DC 20036-1183

This publication was prepared partially with funding from
the Office of Educational Research and Improvement, U.S.
Department of Education, under contract no. ED RI-88-062014.
The opinions expressed in this report do not necessarily
reflect the positions or policies of OERI or the Department.

EXECUTIVE SUMMARY

The use of active learning strategies, such as cooperative learning, is growing at a remarkable rate. Professors are incorpora-
ting cooperative learning to increase students' achievement,
create positive relationships among students, and promote
students' healthy psychological adjustment to school. This
monograph is about how college faculty can ensure that students actively create their knowledge rather than passively
listening to the professor's. It is about structuring learning
situations cooperatively at the college level so that students
work together to achieve shared goals.

What Is Cooperative Learning?

Cooperative learning is the instructional use of small groups
so that students work together to maximize their own and
each other's learning. Considerable research demonstrates
that cooperative learning produces higher achievement, more
positive relationships among students, and healthier psychological adjustment than do competitive or individualistic experiences. These effects, however, do not automatically appear
when students are placed in groups. For cooperative learning
to occur, the professor must carefully structure learning
groups. Further, cooperative learning can be structured in
many different ways. Three broad categories of cooperative
learning strategies are formal cooperative learning groups,
informal cooperative learning groups, and cooperative base
groups. Finally, cooperation can be just as powerful among
faculty as it is among students. To increase faculty members'
effectiveness, the existing competitive/individualistic college
structure must be restructured to a cooperative, team-based
college structure.

The conceptual approach to cooperative learning described
in this monograph involves training professors to apply an
overall system to build cooperative activities, lessons, and
strategies. This conceptual approach is based on a theoretical
framework that provides general principles on how to structure cooperative learning activities in a teacher's specific subject area, curriculum, students, and setting. Using these principles, teachers can analyze their current curricula, students,
and instructional goals, and design appropriate cooperative
lessons. The advantage of conceptual principles is that they
can be used in any classroom, from preschool to graduate
school. The particulars can be adapted for differences in students' age, ability, and background. The appeal of a concep-

tual approach is that it provides a foundation upon which faculty can build. Rather than slavishly following a specific approach, faculty can branch out and try things on their own, using the procedures as models rather than as prescriptives.

Many educators who believe that they are using cooperative learning are, in fact, missing its essence. A crucial difference exists between simply putting students in groups to learn and in structuring cooperation among students. Cooperation is *not* having students sit side by side at the same table to talk with each other as they do their individual assignments. It is *not* assigning a report to a group of students where one student does all the work and the others put their names on the product as well. It is *not* having students do a task individually with instructions that the ones who finish first are to help the slower students. Cooperation is much more than being physically near other students, discussing material with them, helping them, or sharing material among students, although each is important in cooperative learning.

To be cooperative, a group must have clear positive interdependence, members must promote each other's learning and success face to face, hold each other personally and individually accountable to do his or her fair share of the work, use appropriately the interpersonal and small-group skills needed for cooperative efforts to be successful, and process as a group how effectively members are working together. These five essential components must be present for small-group learning to be truly cooperative.

What Are Some Ways to Implement Cooperative Learning?

Cooperative learning groups can be used to teach specific content and problem-solving skills (formal learning groups), ensure active cognitive processing during a lecture (informal learning groups), and provide long-term support and assistance for academic progress (base groups). When used in combination, these learning groups provide an overall structure with variety for students.

Formal cooperative learning groups might last for one class period to several weeks to complete a specific task or assignment. In a cooperative learning group, students work together to accomplish shared goals. They have two responsibilities: to maximize their own learning and to maximize the learning of all the members of the group. First, students receive instructions and objectives from their instructor. Second, the instructor assigns each student to a learning group, provides needed materials, arranges the room, and perhaps gives each student a specific role to fulfill in the group. Third, the instructor explains the task and the cooperative structure. Fourth, the instructor monitors the functioning of each learning group and intervenes to teach cooperative skills and assist in academic learning when needed. Finally, the instructor evaluates the quality and quantity of each student's learning and ensures that each group processes how effectively members are working together. Students who need help in completing the assignment are instructed to ask their peers for assistance first and to request help from the instructor only if needed. Students are expected to interact with members of their group, share ideas and materials, support and encourage each other's academic achievement, orally explain and elaborate the concepts and strategies being learned, and hold each other accountable for completing the assignment, using a criterion-referenced evaluation.

Informal cooperative learning groups are temporary, ad hoc groups that last for only one discussion or one class period. Their purposes are to focus students' attention on the material to be learned, set a mood conducive to learning, help organize in advance the material to be covered in a class session, ensure that students cognitively process the material being taught, and provide closure to an instructional session. They can be used at any time but are especially useful during a lecture or direct teaching before the students' eyes begin to glaze over (some estimate the length of time that people can attend to a lecture to be about 12 to 15 minutes; students then need to process what they are learning or their minds drift away). During direct teaching, the instructional challenge for the teacher is to ensure that students do the intellectual work of organizing material, explaining it, summarizing it, and integrating it into existing conceptual networks, which can be achieved by having students do the advance organizing, cognitively process what they are learning, and summarize their learning. Breaking up lectures with short cooperative processing times gives the instructor slightly less lecture time but enhances what is learned and builds relationships among students. It helps counter what is proclaimed as the main problem of lectures: The information passes from the notes of the professor to the notes of the student without passing through the mind of either one.

Base groups are long-term, heterogeneous cooperative learning groups with stable membership whose primary responsibility is to provide each student the support, encouragement, and assistance needed to progress academically. Base groups personalize the work required and the learning experiences in the course. They consist of three or four participants who stay together during the entire course, perhaps exchanging phone numbers and information about schedules so they can meet outside class.

Why Bother Using Cooperative Learning?
Over 600 studies have been conducted during the past 90 years comparing the effectiveness of cooperative, competitive, and individualistic efforts. These studies have been conducted by a wide variety of researchers in different decades with subjects of different ages, in different subject areas, and in different settings. More is known about the efficacy of cooperative learning than about lecturing, departmentalization, the use of instructional technology, or almost any other aspect of education. The more one works in cooperative learning groups, the more that person learns, the better he understands what he is learning, the easier it is to remember what he learns, and the better he feels about himself, the class, and his classmates.

Cooperative learning, although not the easiest way to teach, can revitalize students and faculty by providing a structured environment for sharing some of the responsibility for learning. Through working together to learn complex conceptual information and master knowledge and skills, students learn more, have more fun, and develop many other skills, such as learning how to work with one another. Faculty, meanwhile, must provide the foundation and learning structures to guide their students in this new learning experience.

ADVISORY BOARD

CONSULTING EDITORS

William E. Becker
Indiana University

Rose R. Bell
New School for Social Research

Louis W. Bender
Florida State University

David G. Brown
University of North Carolina–Asheville

David W. Chapman
State University of New York–Albany

Linda Clement
University of Maryland

James Cooper
FIPSE College Teaching Project

Richard A. Couto
Tennessee State University

Donald F. Dansereau
Texas Christian University

Peter Frederick
Wabash College

Mildred Garcia
Montclair State College

Virginia N. Gordon
Ohio State University

Wesley R. Habley
American College Testing

Dianne Horgan
Memphis State University

Don Hossler
Indiana University

John L. Howarth
Private Consultant

William Ihlanfeldt
Northwestern University

Susan Jeffords
University of Washington

Greg Johnson
Harvard College

Margaret C. King
Schenectady County Community College

Joseph Lowman
University of North Carolina

Jean MacGregor
Evergreen State College

Christine Maitland
National Education Association

Jerry W. Miller
American College Testing

James R. Mingle
State Higher Education Executive Officers

Richard W. Moore
California State University–Northridge

Richard Morrill
Centre College

Laura I. Rendón
North Carolina State University

R. Eugene Rice
Antioch University

Richard Robbins
State University of New York–Plattsburg

Susan Stroud
Brown University

Marilla D. Svinicki
University of Texas–Austin

Elizabeth Watson
California State University–Humboldt

William R. Whipple
University of Maine

Roger B. Winston
University of Georgia

CONTENTS

FOREWORD

The power of cooperative interaction has long been known. In his seminal work on successful people, *Think and Grow Rich,* Napoleon Hill (New York: Hawthorne, 1966) continuously emphasizes that the most effective method for generating creative thinking is to have several people focus cooperatively on the same problem. Hill refers to this technique as the "mastermind method." In a more recent best seller, *Seven Habits of Highly Effective People,* Stephen Covey (New York: Simon & Schuster, 1989) identifies the sixth habit as developing a "synergy" or interdependent relationship between two or more people. Such a group will prove noticeably more productive than the same number of people working individually.

One of the major reasons Japanese businesses are far more successful than those in the United States is their reliance on team effort. If interdependent relationships, team building, and cooperative learning are known to be highly effective in increasing individual productivity, then why is cooperative learning not used more often in higher education?

The answer lies in the cultures of both our society and traditional higher education. The reward system favors individual performance—"doing it on your own"—for students as well as for faculty. Because faculty have been conditioned to respond as individual scholars and have been taught that cooperative activities such as team teaching and joint publications are, on the whole, of low value, they place a low value on developing the cooperative learning skills of their students.

In this report, David W. Johnson, professor of educational psychology, Roger T. Johnson, professor of curriculum and instruction, and Karl A. Smith, associate professor in the Department of Civil and Mineral Engineering, all at the University of Minnesota, explain cooperative learning, the basis for its success as a learning tool, and the techniques for its most effective use. They also discuss in depth the cooperative lecture, cooperative learning structures, informal cooperative learning groups, base groups, and cooperation among faculty. The authors take a how-to approach to the use of cooperative learning, and include descriptions of typical cooperative learning class sessions.

The literature on the effectiveness of interdependent and cooperative interaction clearly demonstrates the importance of developing cooperative learning skills in our students.

Learning these skills will not be easy for faculty or students, because such behavior often runs counter to well-established values. But those institutions that make cooperative learning one of their priorities will find both faculty instructional productivity and students' learning noticeably improved.

Jonathan D. Fife
Series Editor, Professor, and
Director, ERIC Clearinghouse on Higher Education

PREFACE

Numerous approaches to the use of groups in college have been described, including traditional learning groups (Bouton and Garth 1983), learning communities (Gabelnick et al. 1990), collaborative learning (MacGregor 1990; Romer 1985), and peer teaching (Whitman 1988). Summarizing all of these approaches is beyond the scope of this monograph; consequently, it focuses on just one of the many approaches to using groups in college—cooperative learning.

A variety of approaches to cooperative learning exist—all effective and interesting and with more similarities than differences—but most are focused on the elementary school level, with some applications at the secondary level. These approaches can be divided into two different but interrelated ways to train teachers to use cooperative learning: direct and conceptual. The direct approach involves training teachers to use a specific cooperative activity, to teach a specific cooperative lesson, to apply a specific cooperative strategy, and to use a curriculum based on cooperative learning. Some of the most effective strategies include the jigsaw method (Aronson et al. 1978), the coop/coop strategy (Kagan 1988), the group project method (Sharan and Sharan 1976), team-assisted individualization (Slavin 1983, 1990), math groups-of-four (Burns 1987), and tribes (Gibbs 1987).

The conceptual approach involves training teachers to apply an overall conceptual system to build cooperative activities, lessons, and strategies. It is based on a theoretical framework that provides general principles on how to structure cooperative learning activities in a teacher's specific subject area, curriculum, students, and setting. Using these principles, teachers can analyze their current curricula, students, and instructional goals, and design appropriate cooperative lessons. The advantage of conceptual principles is that they can be used in any classroom, from preschool to graduate school. The particulars can be adapted for differences in students' age, ability, and background. The two conceptual approaches to cooperative learning (Cohen 1986; Johnson and R. Johnson 1974, 1991) are based on, respectively, expectation-states theory and the theory of cooperation and competition that Morton Deutsch derived from Kurt Lewin's field theory.

The appeal of a conceptual approach is that it provides a foundation upon which faculty can build. Rather than slavishly following a specific approach, faculty can branch out, using the procedures as models rather than as prescriptives.

ACKNOWLEDGMENTS

Although much has been written about cooperative learning, little is aimed at the college level. Our interest in cooperative learning began in our own classes at the University of Minnesota. Starting in the 1960s, refining ideas in the 1970s, and writing articles about cooperative learning in college in the 1980s, we now believe it is important to synthesize and summarize what is known about cooperative learning in higher education. Jim Cooper is also writing about (and advocating for) cooperative learning at this level (Cooper 1990).

Many colleagues have shared with us their favorite procedures for implementing cooperative learning and have in turn implemented our ideas in their classrooms with great success. We have been in their classrooms and have taught beside them. We appreciate their ideas and celebrate their successes. In addition, we have had many talented and productive graduate students who have conducted research studies that have significantly contributed to our understanding of cooperative learning. We feel privileged to have worked with them.

Our debt to Judy Bartlett is unmeasurable. Her talents, her dedication, and her work beyond the call of duty have all contributed to the completion of this monograph. We are continually impressed with and are grateful for her work. She also believes in cooperative learning and often works beyond the call of duty to ensure that it is shared with students in the classroom.

Finally, we dedicate this monograph to our wives, Linda Mulholland Johnson, Anne Earle Johnson, and Lila Arduser Smith, who help us keep our cooperative skills sharp.

WHAT IS COOPERATIVE LEARNING?

On July 15, 1982, Don Bennett, a Seattle businessman, was the first amputee ever to climb Mount Rainier (Kouzes and Posner 1987). He climbed 14,410 feet on one leg and two crutches. It took him five days. When asked to state the most important lesson he learned from doing so, without hesitation he said, "You can't do it alone."

In every college classroom, no matter what the subject, instructors can structure lessons so that students work collaboratively in small groups, ensuring that all members master the assigned material; engage in a win-lose struggle to see who is best; or work independently on their own, learning goals at their own pace and in their own space to achieve a preset criterion of excellence.

We are currently leaving an era of competitive and individualistic learning. The "me" classrooms and "do your own thing" academic work are fading, and we are entering an era of interdependence and mutuality. The current trend is for "we" classrooms and "we are all in this together" learning. In contrast to fads, which are generated from the top down, trends are generated from the bottom up, and, like horses, they are easier to ride in the direction they are already going. This monograph is about the trend, being set by faculty from all parts of the world, toward using cooperative learning in classrooms from freshman orientation to graduate school.

After half a century of relative neglect, cooperative learning is increasingly used throughout public and private colleges. The intent of this monograph is to provide instructors with the knowledge required to begin to use cooperative learning. To gain this expertise, faculty must first understand what cooperative learning is and how it differs from competitive and individualistic learning. Second, they must be confident that using cooperative learning is the most effective approach to teaching. Confidence in the use of cooperative learning in the college classroom is based on 90 years of research that have produced over 600 studies demonstrating that cooperative learning results in higher achievement, more positive relationships among students, and healthier psychological adjustment than does competitive or individualistic learning. Third, faculty must realize that simply placing students in discussion groups does not magically produce these results. Effective cooperation requires five essential elements structured within the learning experience (discussed in the next section). Fourth, faculty must know that cooperative learning

In essence, the organizational structure of colleges must change from competitive and individualistic to cooperative.

can be used many different ways in the college classroom: formal cooperative learning groups, informal cooperative learning groups, and base groups. Finally, what is good for students is even better for faculty. It is just as important to organize faculty into cooperative teams as it is to use cooperative learning in the classroom. In essence, the organizational structure of colleges must change from competitive and individualistic to cooperative.

During one very difficult trek across an ice field in the hop to the summit of Mount Rainier, Don Bennett's daughter stayed by his side for four hours and with each new hop told him, "You can do it, Dad. You're the best dad in the world. You can do it, Dad." No way would Bennett quit climbing with his daughter yelling words of love and encouragement in his ear. Her encouragement strengthened his commitment to make it to the top and kept him moving forward. College life is like that. With members of their cooperative group cheering them on, students amaze themselves and their instructors with what they can achieve.

Student-Student Interaction

Student-student interaction in college classes can be structured in three ways: competitively, individualistically, and cooperatively. When students are required to compete with each other for grades, they work against each other to achieve a goal that only one or a few students can attain. Students are graded on a norm-referenced basis, requiring them to work faster and more accurately than their peers. In doing so, they strive to be better than classmates and to deprive others (my winning means you lose), to celebrate classmates' failures (your failure makes it easier for me to win), to view grades as limited (only a few of us will get A's), to recognize their negatively linked fate (the more you gain, the less for me, and the more I gain, the less for you), and to believe that more competent and harder-working individuals become haves and less competent and less deserving individuals become the have nots (only the strong prosper). Competitive situations entail a negative interdependence among goals achieved; students perceive that they can obtain their goals if and only if other students in the class fail to obtain their goals (Deutsch 1962; Johnson and R. Johnson 1991). Unfortunately, most students perceive college classes as predominantly competitive enterprises. Students either work hard to do better than their classmates, or they take it easy because they do not believe they have a chance to win.

When students are required to work individualistically on their own, they work by themselves to accomplish goals for learning unrelated to those of other students. Individual goals are assigned, and students' efforts are evaluated on certain criteria. Each student has his or her own set of materials and works at his or her own speed, ignoring the other students in the class. Students are encouraged and expected to focus on their strict self-interest (how well can I do?), to value only their own efforts and success (if I study hard, I can get a high grade), and to ignore as irrelevant the success or failure of others (whether my classmates study or not does not affect me). In individualistic learning situations, the goals students achieve are independent; students perceive that the achievement of their goals for learning is unrelated to what other students do (Deutsch 1962; Johnson and R. Johnson 1991).

Cooperation is working together to accomplish shared goals. When engaged in cooperative activities, individuals seek outcomes that are beneficial to themselves *and* to all other members of the group. Cooperative learning is the instructional use of small groups so that students work together to maximize their own and each other's learning. The idea is simple. Class members are split into small groups after receiving instruction from the teacher. They work through the assignment until all members of the group successfully understand and complete it. Cooperation results in participants' striving for mutual benefit so that all members of the group benefit from each other's efforts (your success benefits me and my success benefits you), their recognizing that all group members share a common fate (we sink or swim together here) and that one's performance depends mutually on oneself and one's colleagues (we cannot do it without you), and their feeling proud and jointly celebrating when a group member is recognized for achievement (you got an A! that's terrific!). Cooperative learning entails a positive interdependence among goals attained; students perceive that they can reach their goals for learning if and only if other students in the learning group also reach their goals (Deutsch 1962; Johnson and R. Johnson 1991).

In every classroom, instructional activities are aimed at accomplishing learning goals and are conducted under a goal structure. A learning goal is a desired future state of demonstrating competence or mastery in the subject area. The goal structure specifies the ways in which students will interact with each other and the teacher. Each goal structure has its place (see Johnson and R. Johnson 1991). In the ideal classroom, all students would learn how to work collaboratively with others, to compete for fun and enjoyment, and to work on their own. The teacher decides which goal structure to implement for each lesson.

Cooperative learning is the most important of the three types of learning situations, yet currently it is the least used in college classrooms. This situation has not always been the case. Cooperative learning is a tradition within education.

The History of Cooperative Learning

> *Two are better than one, because they have a good reward for toil. For if they fall, one will lift up his fellow; but woe to him who is alone when he falls and has not another to lift him up. . . . And though a man might prevail against one who is alone, two will withstand him. A threefold cord is not quickly broken.*
>
> —Ecclesiastes 4:9–12

Cooperative learning is an old idea. The capacity to work cooperatively has been a major contributor to the survival of our species. The Talmud clearly states that to learn, one must have a learning partner. As early as the first century, Quintilian argued that students could benefit from teaching one another. John Amos Comenius (1592–1670) believed that students would benefit by teaching and being taught by other students. In the late 1700s, Joseph Lancaster and Andrew Bell used cooperative learning groups extensively in England, and the idea was brought to the United States when a Lancastrian school was opened in New York City in 1806. The Common School Movement in the United States in the early 1800s emphasized cooperative learning. Certainly, the use of cooperative learning is not new to U.S. education. At certain periods, cooperative learning had strong advocates and was widely used to promote the educational goals of the time.

One of the most successful advocates of cooperative learning in the United States was Colonel Francis Parker. In the last three decades of the 19th century, Colonel Parker brought to his advocacy of cooperative learning enthusiasm, idealism, practicality, and an intense devotion to freedom, democracy, and individuality in the public schools. His fame and success rested on the vivid and regenerating spirit that he brought into the schoolroom and on his power to create a cooperative, democratic classroom atmosphere. When he was superintendent of the public schools in Quincy, Massachusetts (1875–1880), he averaged more than 30,000 visitors a year to examine his use of cooperative learning (Campbell 1965). Parker's instructional methods of promoting cooperation among students dominated U.S. education through the turn of the century. Following Parker, John Dewey promoted the use of cooperative learning groups as part of his famous project method in instruction (Dewey 1916). In the late 1930s, however, interpersonal competition began to be emphasized in public schools and colleges (Pepitone 1980). The authors began their work on cooperative learning in the 1960s, resulting in the formation of the Cooperative Learning Center at the University of Minnesota in the early 1970s. In the 1970s, David DeVries and Keith Edwards began work on cooperative learning at the Johns Hopkins University's Center for Social Organization of Schools. Several groups of researchers and practitioners throughout the United States and Canada and in several other countries are engaged in the study and implementation of cooperative learning and its lessons, curricula, strategies, and procedures.

In addition to the history of its practical use, cooperative learning has a history of theorizing about and researching cooperative, competitive, and individualistic efforts. The research studies began in the late 1800s, when Triplett in the United States, Turner in England, and Mayer in Germany conducted a series of studies on the factors associated with competitive performance. May and Doob (1937) conducted an initial review of the research. In the 1940s, Morton Deutsch, building on the theorizing of Kurt Lewin, proposed a theory of cooperative and competitive situations that has served as the primary foundation on which subsequent research and discussion have been based. The authors' own theorizing and research are based directly on Deutsch's work (Johnson and Johnson 1989a).

Basic Elements of Cooperative Learning

Together we stand, divided we fall.
                    —Watchword of the American Revolution

The instructor is trying out learning groups in a classroom. "This is a mess," she thinks. In one group, students are bickering over who will write the group's conclusions. In another group, a member sits quietly, too shy to participate. Two members of a third group are talking about football, while the third member works on the assignment. "My students do not know how to work cooperatively," the instructor concludes.

What is an instructor to do in such a situation? Simply placing students in groups and telling them to work together does not mean that they know how to cooperate or that they will do so even if they know how. Many instructors believe that they are implementing cooperative learning when in fact they are missing its essence. Putting students into groups to learn is not the same as structuring cooperation among students. Cooperation is not, for example:

1. Having students sit side by side at the same table and talk with each other as they do their individual assignments;
2. Having students do a task individually with instructions that those who finish first are to help the slower students;
3. Assigning a report to a group, with one student doing all the work and others merely putting their names on it.

Cooperation is much more than being physically near other students, discussing material with other students, helping other students, or sharing materials with other students—although each is important in cooperative learning.

For a lesson to be cooperative, five basic elements must be included: positive interdependence, face-to-face promotive interaction, individual accountability, social skills, and group processing (Johnson, Johnson, and Holubec 1990). In a math class, for example, an instructor assigns her students a set of problems to solve. Students are placed in groups of three. The instructional task is for students to solve each problem correctly and understand the correct strategy for doing so. The instructor at this point implements the five basic elements. To implement positive interdependence—of goals, roles, resources, and rewards—students must believe that they are linked with others in a way that one cannot succeed unless the other members of the group succeed (and vice versa); that is, they sink or swim together. Within the lesson, the instructor creates positive goal interdependence (the most important element, for all cooperative learning starts with a mutually shared group goal) by requiring group members to agree on the answer and the strategies for solving each problem. Positive role interdependence is structured by assigning each student a role. For example, the *reader* reads the problems aloud to the group. The *checker* makes sure that all members can explain how to solve each problem correctly. And the *encourager* in a friendly way encourages all members of the group to participate in the discussion, sharing their ideas and feelings. Positive resource interdependence is created by giving each group one copy of the problems to be solved. All students work the problems on scratch paper and share their insights with each other. And positive reward interdependence is structured by giving each group five points if all members score above 90 percent correct on the test given at the end of the unit.

The second element of a cooperative lesson, face-to-face promotive interaction among students, exists when students help, assist, encourage, and support each other's efforts to learn. Students promote each other's learning by orally explaining to each other how to solve problems, by discussing with each other the nature of the concepts and strategies being learned, by teaching their knowledge to each other, and by explaining to each other the connections between present and past learning. In the math lesson in the example, the instructor must provide the time, face-to-face seating arrangement, and encouragement for students to exchange ideas and to help each other learn.

Individual accountability exists when each student's performance is assessed and the results are given back to the group and the individual. Group members must know who needs more assistance in completing the assignment and that they cannot hitchhike on the work of others. Common ways of structuring individual accountability include giving a test to each student and randomly selecting one student's work to represent the efforts of the entire group.

Groups cannot function effectively without social skills, that is, if students do not have and use the needed skills in leadership, making decisions, building trust, communicating, and managing conflict. And these skills must be taught just as purposefully and precisely as academic skills. Many students have never worked cooperatively in learning situations and therefore lack the needed social skills for doing so. In the math lesson in the example, the instructor emphasizes the skill of "checking to make sure everyone understands," defining the skill as the phrases and the accompanying nonverbal behaviors the checker is to use. The group's roles are rotated each day. When the instructor sees students engaging in the skill, she verbally praises the group and/or records the instance on an observation sheet. (Procedures and strategies for teaching students social skills can be found in Johnson [1990, 1991], Johnson and F. Johnson [1991], and Johnson, Johnson, and Holubec [1990].)

Finally, the instructor must ensure that groups process how well they are achieving their goals and maintaining effective working relationships among members. At the end of the math period, the groups process their functioning by answering two questions: (1) What is something each member did that was helpful for the group, and (2) What is something each member could do to make the group even better tomorrow? Such processing enables learning groups to focus on maintaining the group, facilitates the learning of social skills, ensures that members receive feedback on their participation, and reminds students to practice the small-group skills required to work cooperatively. Successful processing includes:

1. Allowing sufficient time for it to occur
2. Making it specific rather than vague
3. Varying the format
4. Maintaining students' involvement in processing
5. Reminding students to use their social skills in processing
6. Ensuring that expectations of the purpose of processing have been clearly communicated.

Often, each group is required to turn in a summary of the processing that all group members must sign.

These five elements are what differentiates cooperative learning groups from traditional discussion groups and a well-structured cooperative learning lesson from a poorly structured one. (See the next section for more detail about the five basic elements.) Three broad types of cooperative learning groups are structured through the use of these five basic elements.

Types of Cooperative Learning Groups

These problems are endemic to all institutions of education, regardless of level. Children sit for 12 years in classrooms where the implicit goal is to listen to the teacher and memorize the information in order to regurgitate it on a test. Little or no attention is paid to the learning process, even though much research exists documenting that real understanding is a case of active restructuring on the part of the learner. Restructuring occurs through engagement in problem posing as well as problem solving, inference making and investigation, resolving of contradictions, and reflecting. These processes all mandate far more active learners, as well as a different model of education, than the one subscribed to at present by most institutions. Rather than being powerless and dependent on the institution, learners need to be empowered to think and learn for themselves. Thus, learning needs to be conceived of as something a learner does, not something that is done to a learner (Fosnot 1989).

Students often feel helpless and discouraged, especially when facing a difficult class or when they have just entered college. Giving them partners in cooperative learning provides hope and opportunity. An important objective of college instructors' use of cooperative learning is empowering students by organizing them into cooperative teams. It is social support from and accountability to valued peers that motivate committed efforts to achieve and succeed. Cooperative learning groups empower their members by making them feel strong, capable, and committed. If classrooms are to be places where students care about each other and are committed to each other's success in academic endeavors, a cooperative structure must exist. Such a cooperative structure consists of the integrated use of three types of cooperative learning groups: formal, informal, and base groups.

Cooperative learning groups can be used to teach specific content (formal cooperative learning groups), to ensure active cognitive processing of information during a lecture (informal cooperative learning groups), and to provide long-term support and assistance for academic progress (cooperative base groups). Any assignment in any curriculum can be done cooperatively. In formal cooperative learning groups, the instructor structures the learning groups (deciding the size of groups and who is assigned to them), teaches the academic concepts, principles, and strategies that students are to master and apply, assigns a task to be completed cooperatively, monitors the learning groups' functioning and intervenes to teach collaborative skills and assist in academic learning when needed, evaluates students' learning, and guides learning groups' processing of their effectiveness.

During a lecture, informal cooperative learning groups can focus students' attention on the material to be learned, set a mood conducive to learning, help set expectations about what will be covered in a class session, ensure that students cognitively process the material being taught, and provide closure to an instructional session. Students can summarize in three- to five-minute discussions what they know about a topic in focused discussions before and after a lecture. Short three- to five-minute discussions in cooperative pairs can be interspersed throughout a lecture, thus countering the main problem of lectures: The information passes from the notes of the professor to the notes of the student without passing through the mind of either one.

Finally, cooperative base groups can be used to provide each student the support, encouragement, and assistance he or she needs to progress academically. Base groups meet daily (or whenever the class meets). They are permanent (lasting from one to several years) and provide the long-term caring relationships among peers necessary to influence members consistently to work hard in college. The use of base groups tends to improve attendance, to personalize the work required and the school experience, and to improve the quality and quantity of learning. The larger the class or college and the more complex and difficult the subject matter, the more important base groups are.

When used in combination, cooperative formal, informal, and base groups provide an overall structure for learning in college.

Back to the Basics

Everyone has to work together; if we can't get everybody working toward common goals, nothing is going to happen.
—Harold K. Sperlich, president, Chrysler Corporation

The importance of cooperative learning goes beyond maximizing outcomes like achievement, positive attitudes toward subject areas, and the ability to think critically—although these outcomes are certainly worthwhile. Knowledge and skills are of little use if a student cannot apply them in cooperative interaction with other people. It does no good to train an engineer, accountant, or teacher if the person does not have the cooperative skills needed to apply the knowledge and technical skills in cooperative relationships on the job. A recent survey emphasizes learning to learn; listening and oral communication; competence in reading, writing, and computation; adaptability based on creative thinking and problem solving; personal management characterized by self-esteem, motivation to set goals, and personal/career development; group effectiveness characterized by interpersonal skills, negotiation skills, and teamwork; and organizational effectiveness and leadership (American Society 1988).

Much of what students have traditionally learned in school is worthless in the real world. Schools teach that work means performing tasks largely by oneself, that helping others is cheating, that technical competencies are the only things that matter, that attendance and punctuality are secondary to test scores, that motivation is up to the teacher, that success depends on performance on individual tests, and that promotions are granted no matter how little one works. In the real world of work, things are altogether different. Most employers do not expect people to sit in rows and compete with colleagues without interacting with them. The heart of most jobs, especially the higher-paying, more interesting jobs, is teamwork, which involves getting others to cooperate, leading others, coping with complex issues of power and influence, and helping solve people's problems by working with them. Teamwork, communication, effective coordination, and division of labor characterize most real-life settings. Grades in school do not predict success in a career. Social skills do. It is time for schools to leave the ivory tower of working alone and sitting in rows and more realistically reflect the realities of adult life.

Students increasingly live in a world characterized by interdependence, pluralism, conflict, and rapid change. Because of technological, economic, ecological, and political interdependence, the solution to most problems cannot be achieved by one country alone. The major problems we face

Grades in school do not predict success in a career. Social skills do.

(contamination of the environment, global warming, world hunger, violence toward women and children, and international terrorism, for example) are increasingly ones that cannot be solved by actions taken only at the national level. Our students will live in a complex, interconnected world where cultures collide every minute and dependencies limit the flexibility of individuals and nations. The internationalization of problems will increase, and no clear division will exist between domestic and international problems. Students need to learn the competencies necessary to manage interdependence, resolve conflicts within cooperative systems comprised of parties from different countries and cultures, and personally adapt to rapid change.

Quality of life depends on having close friends who last a lifetime, building and maintaining a loving family, being a responsible parent, caring about others, and contributing to the world's well-being. These things make life worthwhile. Grades in school do not predict which students will attain a high quality of life after they graduate. The ability to work cooperatively with others does. Students' ability to work collaboratively with others is the keystone to building and maintaining the caring and committed relationships that largely determine quality of life.

Summary
Cooperative learning is the instructional use of small groups so that students work together to maximize their own and each other's learning. Considerable research demonstrates that cooperative learning produces higher achievement, more positive relationships among students, and healthier psychological adjustment than do competitive or individualistic experiences. These effects, however, do not automatically appear when students are placed in groups. To be cooperative, learning groups must be carefully structured. Further, cooperative learning can be structured in many different ways. And cooperation is just as powerful among faculty as it is among students. The organization of the existing competitive, individualistic college structure must be re-formed to a cooperative, team-based college structure.

Each of these topics is discussed in detail in this monograph. The next section discusses the five basic elements, the third focuses on the research and theory underlying the engineering of cooperation within colleges, the next three deal specifically with the three types of cooperative learning groups, the seventh discusses cooperation among faculty, and the final section summarizes and concludes the topic.

BASIC ELEMENTS OF COOPERATIVE LEARNING

When Cooperation Fails

Aesop tells a story of a man who had four sons. The father loved them very much, but they troubled him greatly, for they were always fighting with each other. Nothing the father said stopped their quarreling. "What can I do to show my sons how wrong it is to act this way?" the father thought. One day he called his sons to him and showed them a bundle of sticks. "Which of you, my sons, can break this bundle of sticks?" he asked them. All the boys tried in turn, but not one of them could do it. Then the father untied the bundle and gave each son a single stick. "See if you can break that," he said. Of course, they could easily do it. "My sons," the father said, "each of you alone is weak. He is as easy to injure as one of these sticks. But if you will be friends and stick together, you will be as strong as the bundle of sticks."

Cooperation pervades all aspects of our lives—which does not mean that it is easy to learn to cooperate. Cooperation often goes wrong because of a lack of understanding of the critical elements that mediate its effectiveness. Simply placing individuals in groups and telling them to work together does not in and of itself promote higher achievement and greater productivity. Group efforts can be ineffective in many ways. Less able members sometimes leave it to others to complete the group's tasks, thus creating the "free-rider effect" (Kerr and Bruun 1983) in which group members expend decreasing amounts of effort and just go through the motions of team-work. At the same time, more able group members might expend less effort to avoid the "sucker effect" of doing all the work (Kerr 1983). Group members with high ability might be deferred to and take over the important leadership roles in ways that benefit them at the expense of the other group members (the "rich-get-richer effect"). In a learning group, for example, abler group members might give all the explanations of what is being learned. Because the amount of time spent explaining correlates highly with the amount learned, abler members learn a great deal, while less able members flounder as a captive audience. The time spent listening in group brainstorming sessions can reduce the amount of time any individual can state his or her ideas (Hill 1982; Lamm and Trommsdorff 1973). A group's efforts can be characterized by self-induced helplessness (Langer and Benevento 1978), diffusion of responsibility and social loafing (Latane, Williams, and Harkins 1979), ganging up against a task, reactance

(Salomon 1981), dysfunctional divisions of labor ("I'm the thinkist and you're the typist") (Sheingold, Hawkins, and Char 1984), inappropriate dependence on authority (Webb, Ender, and Lewis 1986), destructive conflict (Collins 1970; Johnson and Johnson 1979), and other patterns of behavior that debilitate the group's performance.

It is only under certain conditions that cooperative efforts can be expected to be more productive than competitive and individualistic efforts:

1. Clearly perceived positive interdependence;
2. Considerable promotive (face-to-face) interaction;
3. Clearly perceived individual accountability and personal responsibility to achieve the group's goals;
4. Frequent use of the relevant interpersonal and small-group skills;
5. Frequent and regular group processing of current functioning to improve the group's future effectiveness.

Positive Interdependence

All for one and one for all.

—Alexandre Dumas

In a football game, the quarterback who throws a pass and the receiver who catches it are positively interdependent. The success of one depends on the success of the other: It takes two to complete a pass. One player cannot succeed without the other, and both have to perform competently if their mutual success is to be assured. They sink or swim together.

The first requirement for an effectively structured cooperative lesson is that students believe that they sink or swim together. In cooperative learning situations, students have two responsibilities: to learn the assigned material and to ensure that all members of the group learn the assigned material. The technical term for this dual responsibility is "positive interdependence." Positive interdependence exists when students perceive that they are linked with other members of the group in a way that they cannot succeed unless the other members do (and vice versa) and/or that they must coordinate their efforts with the efforts of the others to complete a task. Positive interdependence promotes a situation in which students (1) see that their work benefits other members of the group and other members' work benefits them and (2) work together in small groups to maximize the learning of all members by sharing their resources, providing mutual support and encouragement, and celebrating their joint successes. Clearly understood, positive interdependence highlights (1) that each group member's efforts are required and indispensable for the group's success (there can be no free riders), and (2) that each group member has a distinctive contribution to make to the joint effort because of his or her resources and/or role and responsibilities.

Positive interdependence can be structured in a number of ways within a learning group:

1. *Positive goal interdependence*—To ensure that students believe they sink or swim together and care about how much each other learns, the instructor must structure a clear group or mutual goal, such as "learn the assigned material and make sure that all members of your group learn the assigned material." The group's goal always has to be part of the lesson.

2. *Positive reward/celebration interdependence*—To supplement goal interdependence, the instructor might want to add joint rewards (if all members of the group score 90 percent or better on the test, each will receive five bonus points). Sometimes instructors give students a group grade for the group's overall production, individual grades resulting from tests, and bonus points if all members of the group achieve up to the criterion on the tests. Regular celebrations of the group's efforts and successes enhance the quality of cooperation.

3. *Positive resource interdependence*—The instructor might highlight cooperative relationships by giving students limited resources that must be shared (one copy of the problem or task per group) or giving each student part of the required resources that the group must then fit together (the jigsaw procedure).

4. *Positive role interdependence*—The instructor creates role interdependence among students by assigning them complementary roles, such as reader, recorder, checker (of understanding), encourager (of participation), and elaborator (of knowledge). Such roles are vital to high-quality learning. The role of checker, for example, focuses on periodically asking each member of the group to explain

what is being learned. A large body of well-controlled research on the effectiveness of teaching at the precollegiate level found "checking for comprehension" to be one specific teaching behavior that was significantly associated with higher levels of learning and achievement for students (Rosenshine and Stevens 1986). While the instructor cannot continually check every student's understanding (especially if the class has 300 students), the instructor can engineer such checking by having students work in cooperative groups and assigning one member the role of checker.

A series of studies investigating the nature of positive interdependence and the relative power of the different types of positive interdependence indicate that positive interdependence provides the context within which promotive interaction takes place, that membership in a group and interpersonal interaction among students do not produce higher achievement unless positive interdependence is clearly structured, that the combination of goal and reward interdependence increases achievement over goal interdependence alone, and that resource interdependence does not increase achievement unless goal interdependence is present also (Hwong et al. 1990; Johnson et al. *In press;* Johnson et al. 1990; Lew et al. 1986a, 1986b; Mesch, Johnson, and Johnson 1988; Mesch et al. 1986).

Face-to-Face Promotive Interaction

In an industrial organization, it's the group effort that counts. There's really no room for stars in an industrial organization. You need talented people, but they can't do it alone. They have to have help.
—John F. Donnelly, president, Donnelly Mirrors

Positive interdependence results in promotive interaction, that is, individuals encouraging and facilitating each other's efforts to achieve, complete tasks, and produce to reach the group's goals. While positive interdependence in and of itself could have some effect on outcomes, it is the face-to-face promotive interaction among individuals fostered by positive interdependence that most powerfully influences efforts to achieve, caring and committed relationships, psychological adjustment, and social competence. Promotive interaction is characterized by individuals' helping each other efficiently and effectively, exchanging needed resources (information and materials) and processing information more efficiently and effectively, providing each other with feedback to improve their subsequent performance of their assigned tasks and responsibilities, challenging each other's conclusions and reasoning to promote higher-quality decision making and greater insight into the problems being considered, advocating the exertion of effort to achieve mutual goals, influencing each other's efforts to achieve the group's goals, acting in trusting and trustworthy ways, being motivated to strive for mutual benefit, and achieving a moderate level of arousal characterized by low anxiety and stress. (The research concerning promotive interaction is discussed in some detail in the next section.)

Individual Accountability and Personal Responsibility

What children can do together today, they can do alone tomorrow (Vygotsky 1978).

The early settlers of the Virginia colony at Jamestown had a saying, "If you do not work, you do not eat." Everyone had to do his or her fair share of the work. The third essential element of cooperative learning is individual accountability, which exists when the performance of each student is assessed, the results are given back to the individual and the group, and the student is held responsible by other members of the group for contributing a fair share to the group's success. The group must know who needs more assistance, support, and encouragement in completing the assignment. It is also important that group members know they cannot hitch-hike on the work of others. When it is difficult to identify members' contributions, when members' contributions are redundant, and when members are not responsible for the final outcome, members sometimes seek a free ride—or "social loafing" (Harkins and Petty 1982; Ingham et al. 1974; Kerr and Bruun 1983; Latane, Williams, and Harkins 1979; Moede 1927; Petty et al. 1977; Williams 1981; Williams, Harkins, and Latane 1981).

The purpose of cooperative learning groups is to make each member a stronger individual in his or her own right. Individual accountability is the key to ensuring that all group members are in fact strengthened by learning cooperatively. After participating in a cooperative lesson, group members should be better prepared to complete similar tasks by themselves.

To ensure that each student is individually accountable to do his or her fair share of the group's work, the instructor needs to assess how much effort each member is contributing to the group's work, provide feedback to groups and individual students, help groups avoid redundant efforts by members, and ensure that every member is responsible for the final outcome. Individual accountability can be structured in several common ways:

1. Keeping the size of the group small. The smaller the group, the greater individual accountability could be.
2. Giving an individual test to each student.
3. Examining students orally by randomly calling on one student to present his or her group's work to you (in the presence of the group) or to the entire class.
4. Observing each group and recording the frequency with which each member contributes to the group's work.
5. Assigning one student in each group the role of checker, who then asks other group members to explain the reasoning and rationale underlying the group's answers.
6. Having students teach what they learned to someone else. When all students do so, it is called "simultaneous explaining."

Classroom learning involves a pattern. First, students learn knowledge, skills, strategies, or procedures in a cooperative group. Second, students apply the knowledge or perform the skill, strategy, or procedure alone to demonstrate their personal mastery of the material.

Social Skills

I will pay more for the ability to deal with people than any other ability under the sun.
—John D. Rockefeller

The fourth essential element of cooperative learning is the appropriate use of interpersonal and small-group skills. To coordinate efforts to achieve mutual goals, students must get to know and trust each other, communicate accurately and unambiguously, accept and support each other, and resolve conflicts constructively (Johnson 1990, 1991; Johnson and F. Johnson 1991). Placing socially unskilled students in a group and telling them to cooperate does not guarantee that they will be able to do so effectively. We are not born knowing instinctively how to interact effectively with others. Interpersonal and small-group skills do not magically appear when they are needed. Students must be taught the social skills required for high-quality collaboration and be motivated to use them if cooperative groups are to be productive. The whole field of group dynamics is based on the premise that social skills are the keys to a group's productivity (Johnson and F. Johnson 1991).

The more socially skilled students are and the more attention instructors pay to teaching and rewarding the use of social skills, the higher the achievement that can be expected from cooperative learning groups. Studies on the long-term implementation of cooperative learning investigated the impact of a reward contingent on using social skills as well as positive interdependence and on academic achievement based on performance within cooperative learning groups (Lew et al. 1986a, 1986b; Mesch, Johnson, and Johnson 1988; Mesch et al. 1986). Students were trained weekly in four social skills, and each member of a cooperative group was given two bonus points toward the quiz grade if the teacher observed all group members demonstrating three out of four cooperative skills. The results indicated that the combination of positive interdependence, an academic reward for high performance by all group members, and a reward for social skills promoted the highest achievement.

One way to define a social skill for students is through the use of a T-chart; that is:

1. Write the name of the skill to be learned and practiced at the top of the chart and draw a large T below it;
2. Label the left side of the T "Looks Like" and the right side "Sounds Like";
3. Think of an example for each column and write them below the crossbar;
4. Ask students for other behaviors that the skill involves and list them on the left side;

We are not born knowing instinctively how to interact effectively with others.

5. Ask students for other phrases that exemplify the skill and list them on the right side;
6. Have group members practice both "Looks Like" and "Sounds Like";
7. Observe the groups' work on a lesson and record the frequency with which the skill is used in each group.

Group Processing

Take care of each other. Share your energies with the group. No one must feel alone, cut off, for that is when you do not make it.
—Willi Unsoeld, renowned mountain climber

The fifth essential component of cooperative learning is group processing. Effective group work is influenced by whether or not groups reflect on (i.e., process) how well they are functioning. A process is an identifiable sequence of events taking place over time, and a "process goal" refers to the sequence of events instrumental in achieving outcome goals (Johnson and F. Johnson 1991). Group processing can be defined as reflecting on a group session to describe what actions of the members were helpful and unhelpful and to decide what actions to continue or change. The purpose of group processing is to clarify and improve the effectiveness of the members in contributing to the collaborative efforts to achieve the group's goals.

The results of an examination of the impact on achievement of (1) cooperative learning in which members discussed how well their group was functioning and how they could improve its effectiveness, (2) cooperative learning without any group processing, and (3) individualistic learning indicate that the high-, medium-, and low-achieving students in the cooperation-with-group-processing option achieved higher on measures of daily achievement, postinstructional achievement, and retention than did the students in the other two groups (Yager, Johnson, and Johnson 1985). Students in the cooperation-without-group-processing option achieved higher on all three measures than did the students involved in individualistic learning. A follow-up study comparing cooperative learning without processing, cooperative learning with the instructor's processing (that is, the instructor specified cooperative skills to use, observed, and gave feedback to the whole class as to how well students were using the skills), cooperative learning with processing by instructor and students (the instructor specified cooperative skills to use, observed, gave feedback to the whole class as to how well students were using the skills, and had learning groups discuss how well they interacted as a group), and individualistic learning. Forty-nine high-ability African-American high school seniors and entering college freshmen at Xavier University participated in the study. Students were given a complex problem to solve using a computer. All three cooperative groups performed higher than the students performing individualistically. The combination of processing by teacher and students resulted in greater success in solving the problem than the other cooperative options (Johnson et al. 1990).

While the instructor systematically observes the cooperative learning groups, he or she can learn what students do and do not understand as they explain to each other how to complete the assignment. Listening in on students' explanations provides valuable information about how well students understand the instructions, the major concepts and strategies being learned, and the basic elements of cooperative learning. A three-year study of ways to improve teaching conducted as part of a college faculty development program found that, both faculty and students agreed, faculty needed help in knowing whether the class understood the material (Wilson 1987, p. 18). Listening to students explain how to complete the assignment to members of the group provides better information about what students do and do not know than correct answers on a test or homework assignments handed in.

Processing takes place at two levels—in small groups and in the whole class. To ensure that small-group processing takes place, instructors allocate some time at the end of each class session for each cooperative group to process how effectively members worked together. Groups need to describe what actions of the members were helpful and unhelpful in completing the group's work and decide what behaviors to continue or change. Such processing (1) enables learning groups to focus on maintaining good working relationships among members, (2) facilitates the learning of cooperative skills, (3) ensures that members receive feedback on their participation, (4) ensures that students think on the metacognitive as well as the cognitive level, and (5) provides the means to celebrate the success of the group and reinforce the positive behaviors of group members. Some keys to successful small-group processing are allowing sufficient time for it to take place, providing a structure for processing (such as "list three things your group is doing well today and one thing you could improve"), emphasizing positive feedback, making the processing specific rather than general, maintaining students' involvement in processing, reminding students to use their cooperative skills while they process, and communicating clear expectations about the purpose of processing.

In addition to small-group processing, the instructor should periodically engage in whole-class processing. When cooperative learning groups are used, the teacher observes the groups, analyzes the problems they have working together, and gives feedback to each group on how well its members are working together. The instructor moves from group to group and observes them at work, perhaps using a formal observation sheet to gather specific data on each group. At the end of the class period, the instructor can then conduct a whole-class processing session by sharing with the class the results of the observations. If each group has a peer observer, the results of his or her observations can be added together to get data on the overall class.

An important aspect of both small-group and whole-class processing is group and class celebrations. Feeling successful, appreciated, and respected builds commitment to learning, enthusiasm about working in cooperative groups, and a sense of self-efficacy in terms of mastering the subject matter and working cooperatively with classmates.

Conclusions

Many educators who believe that they are using cooperative learning are, in fact, missing its essence. A crucial difference exists between simply putting students in groups to learn and structuring cooperation among students. Cooperation is not having students sit side by side at the same table to talk with each other as they do their individual assignments. Cooperation is not assigning a report to a group of students in which one student does all the work and the others put their names on the product as well. Cooperation is not having students do a task individually with instructions that the ones who finish first are to help the slower students. Cooperation is much more than being physically near other students, discussing material with other students, helping other students, or sharing material among students—although each of these factors is important in cooperative learning.

To be cooperative, a group must have clear positive interdependence and members must promote each other's learning and success face to face, hold each other individually accountable to do his or her fair share of the work, appropriately use the interpersonal and small-group skills needed for cooperative efforts to be successful, and process as a group how effectively members are working together (see table 1). These five essential components must be present for small-group learning to be truly cooperative.

TABLE 1

WHAT IS THE DIFFERENCE?

Cooperative Learning Groups	Traditional Learning Groups
Positive interdependence	No interdependence
Individual accountability	No individual accountability
Heterogeneous membership	Homogeneous membership
Shared leadership	One appointed leader
Responsible for each other	Responsible only for self
Task and maintenance emphasized	Only task emphasized
Social skills directly taught	Social skills assumed or ignored
Teacher observes and intervenes	Teacher ignores groups
Group processing occurs	No group processing

These five essential elements must be structured within three types of cooperative learning groups: formal, informal, and base groups. Before the three types are discussed in depth, however, it is first necessary to detail why cooperative learning should be used. The next section therefore reviews the research validating the effectiveness of cooperative learning in college classrooms.

RESEARCH ON COOPERATIVE LEARNING

The best answer to the question "What is the most effective method of teaching?" is that it depends on the goal, the students, the content, and the teacher. But the next best answer is, "Students teaching other students." A wealth of evidence suggests that peer teaching is extremely effective for a wide range of goals, content, and students (McKeachie et al. 1986, p. 63).

A professor at the University of Minnesota in his introductory astronomy classes of 300 to 500 students randomly assigns students to groups of four. He provides explicit directions about students' group work and maintains an extensive file system to pass information between the students and the instructor. After students become accustomed to working in groups, he often differentiates assigned roles and assigns each group member one of the roles. The recorder records the group's work by writing out the steps for solving each astronomy problem assigned. The checker makes sure that all members can explain how to solve each problem correctly (or can give an appropriate rationale for the group's answer). The encourager in a friendly way encourages all members of the group to participate in the discussion, sharing their ideas and feelings. The elaborator relates present to past learning.

Within the lesson, positive interdependence is structured by the group's agreeing on the answer and the process for solving each problem. Because the group certifies that each member has the correct answer written on the answer sheet and can correctly explain how to solve each problem, individual accountability is structured by having the professor randomly ask one group member to explain how to solve one of the problems. The cooperative skills emphasized in the lesson are checking, encouraging, and elaborating. Finally, at the end of the period, the groups process how well they are functioning by answering two questions: (1) What is something each member did that was helpful for the group, and (2) What is something each member could do to make the group even better tomorrow?

As a result of structuring this introductory astronomy lesson cooperatively, what instructional outcomes can the professor expect?

Research on Social Interdependence
Learning together to complete assignments can profoundly affect students, teaching assistants, and professors. A great deal

of research has compared the relative effects of cooperative, competitive, and individualistic efforts on instructional outcomes (Johnson and Johnson 1974, 1978, 1983, 1989a; Johnson, Johnson, and Maruyama 1983; Johnson et al. 1981; Pepitone 1980; Sharan 1980; Slavin 1983). Such research began in the late 1800s with a series of studies on the factors associated with competitive performance. The amount of research that has been conducted since is staggering. During the past 90 years, over 575 experimental and 100 correlational studies have been conducted by a wide variety of researchers in different decades with different age subjects, in different subject areas, and in different settings (see Johnson and Johnson 1989a for a complete list of these studies). The research program at the Cooperative Learning Center at the University of Minnesota over the past 25 years has conducted over 85 studies to refine the understanding of how cooperation works. Far more is known about the efficacy of cooperative learning than about lecturing, departmentalization, the use of technology, or almost any other facet of education (see Johnson and Johnson 1989a for a comprehensive review of all studies and meta-analyses of the results).[1]

Building on the theorizing of Kurt Lewin and Morton Deutsch, one can make the premise that the type of interdependence structured among students determines how they interact with each other, which in turn largely determines instructional outcomes. This section is organized around this progression from goal structures to patterns of interaction to outcomes. Structuring situations cooperatively results in promotive interaction, structuring situations competitively results in oppositional interaction, and structuring situations individualistically results in no interaction among students. The characteristics of these three types of social interdependence are summarized in table 2. These patterns of interaction affect numerous variables, which can be subsumed within three broad and interrelated outcomes: effort exerted to achieve,

---

1. This section summarizes the basic results from the meta-analyses on all the studies conducted up to 1989. In addition, separate meta-analyses have been conducted on the results of the 137 experimental studies that compare cooperative, competitive, and individualistic efforts at the college and adult levels. In most cases, references to individual studies are not included in this section. Rather, the reader is referred to the reviews that contain the references to the specific studies that corroborate the point being made.

TABLE 2

CHARACTERISTICS OF SOCIAL INTERDEPENDENCE

Characteristic	Interdependence		
	Positive	Negative	None
Fate	Mutual	Negatively Linked	Individual
Benefit	Mutual	Differential	Self
Time Perspective	Long-Term	Short-Term	Short-Term
Identity	Shared	Relative	Individual
Causation	Mutual	Relative	Self
Affiliation Motives	Enhance	Oppose	Oppose

quality of relationships among participants, and participants' psychological adjustment and social competence (see figure 1) (Johnson and Johnson 1989a).

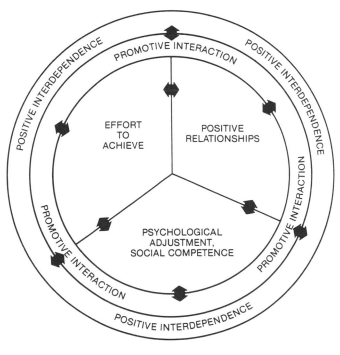

FIGURE 1

OUTCOMES OF COOPERATION

Source: Johnson and Johnson 1989a.

Patterns of Interaction

Two heads are better than one.

Simply placing students near each other and allowing them to interact does not mean that learning will be maximized, high-quality peer relationships will result, or students' psychological adjustment, self-esteem, and social competencies will be enhanced. Students can obstruct as well as facilitate each other's learning. Or they can ignore each other. The way students interact depends on how faculty members structure interdependence in learning.

Positive interdependence results in students' promoting each other's learning and achievement. Promotive interaction is defined as individuals encouraging and facilitating each other's efforts to achieve, complete tasks, and produce to reach the group's goals. While positive interdependence in and of itself might have some effect on outcomes, it is the face-to-face promotive interaction among individuals, fostered by the positive interdependence, that most powerfully influences efforts to achieve, caring and committed relationships, and psychological adjustment and social competence. Students focus on increasing their own achievement and on increasing the achievement of the other members of the group. Promotive interaction is characterized by individuals':

1. Providing each other with efficient and effective assistance;
2. Exchanging needed resources, such as information and materials, and processing information more efficiently and effectively;
3. Providing each other with feedback to improve their subsequent performance of their assigned tasks and responsibilities;
4. Challenging each other's conclusions and reasoning to promote higher-quality decision making and greater insight into the problems being considered;
5. Advocating the exertion of effort to achieve mutual goals;
6. Influencing each other's efforts to achieve the group's goals;
7. Being motivated to strive for mutual benefit;
8. Acting in trusting and trustworthy ways;
9. Exhibiting a moderate level of arousal characterized by low anxiety and stress (Johnson and Johnson 1989a).

Negative interdependence typically results in students' opposing and obstructing each other's learning. Oppositional interaction occurs as students discourage and obstruct each other's efforts to achieve. Students focus on increasing their own achievement and on preventing any classmate from achieving higher than they do. No interaction exists when students work independently without any interaction or interchange with each other. Students focus only on increasing their own achievement and ignore as irrelevant the efforts of others.

Giving and receiving assistance

Within most tasks, productivity is enhanced when individuals give each other relevant task-related help and assistance (Johnson and Johnson 1989a). Cooperative situations contain more consistent perceptions of more frequent helping and tutoring (including cross-ethnic and cross-handicap helping) than competitive or individualistic situations. In research on both social-psychological and applied behavior, cooperative structures have enhanced helping among group members, while competitive structures have resulted in individuals' obstructing each other's efforts to achieve, refusing to help and share, and engaging in antisocial behaviors. These effects of competition are exacerbated by losing. Observational studies of actual learning groups consistently find students giving and receiving more help in cooperative than in competitive or individualistic situations.

Information exchange and cognitive processes

More efficient and effective exchange and processing of information take place in cooperative than in competitive or individualistic situations (Johnson 1974; Johnson and Johnson 1989a). While a wide variety of resources might need to be exchanged to complete tasks and accomplish goals, the most common resource shared and exchanged within cooperative efforts is information.

Compared with competitive and individualistic situations, students working cooperatively:

1. Seek significantly more information from each other than do students working within a competitive goal structure;
2. Are less biased and have fewer misperceptions in comprehending the viewpoints and positions of other individuals;

Oppositional interaction occurs as students discourage and obstruct each other's efforts to achieve.

3. More accurately communicate information by verbalizing ideas and information more frequently, attending to others' statements more carefully, and accepting others' ideas and information more frequently;
4. Are more confident about the value of their ideas;
5. Make optimal use of the information provided by other students (Johnson and Johnson 1989a).

In cooperative situations, students are bound together by their mutual fate, shared identity, and mutual causation, and they therefore celebrate (and feel benefited by) each other's successes. Relevant ideas, information, conclusions, and resources tend to be made available, exchanged, and used in ways that promote collective and individual insights and increase energy to complete the task. Such oral discussion of relevant information has at least two dimensions—oral explanation and listening—and both benefit the giver and the receiver. The giver benefits from the cognitive organizing and processing, higher-level reasoning, insights, and personal commitment to achieving the group's goals derived from orally explaining, elaborating, and summarizing information and teaching one's knowledge to others. The receiver benefits from the opportunity to use others' resources in accomplishing his or her goals.

Exchanging information and stimulating cognitive processes might not occur in competitive or individualistic situations. In competitive situations, the exchange of communication and information tends to be nonexistent or misleading, and competition biases a person's perceptions and comprehension of others' viewpoints and positions. Individualistic situations are usually deliberately structured to ensure that individuals do not communicate or exchange information at all.

Survey research indicates that fear of public speaking is quite common among the general population of adolescents and adults (Motley 1988). College students in particular are frequently apprehensive about speaking in the classroom (Bowers 1986). Such anxiety, however, can be significantly reduced if students are given the opportunity to first express themselves in the more comfortable social context of a small group of peers (Neer 1987). Students whose primary language is not English could especially find anxiety reduced by working in small groups in college classes.

Peer feedback

An important aspect of promotive interaction is the opportunity for group members to provide each other with feedback about how they are fulfilling their responsibilities and completing their work. Feedback is information made available to individuals that makes possible the comparison of actual performance with some standard of performance. Knowledge of results is information provided to the person about his or her performance on a given effort. It could be in the form of qualitative information in which the person is informed that a performance is either correct or incorrect. Or it could be quantitative information about how much discrepancy exists between the person's response and the correct response. Usually, quantitative information (that is, process feedback) about the size of the discrepancy existing between actual performance and some standard of performance or how to improve one's reasoning or performance promotes achievement more effectively than qualitative information (that is, terminal feedback) about being right or wrong or what the correct answer is. Receiving personalized feedback from another person increases performance to a greater extent than does receiving impersonal feedback; peer feedback from collaborators could be especially vivid and personalized. Frequent and immediate feedback increases a student's motivation to learn (Mackworth 1970).

Challenge and controversy

An important aspect of promotive interaction is controversy, the conflict that arises when involved group members have different information, perceptions, opinions, reasoning processes, theories, and conclusions and must reach agreement. When controversies arise, they can be dealt with constructively or destructively, depending on how they are managed and the level of interpersonal and small-group skills of the participants. When managed constructively, controversy promotes uncertainty about the correctness of one's views, an active search for more information, a reconceptualization of one's knowledge and conclusions, and, consequently, greater mastery and retention of the material being discussed. Individuals working alone in competitive and individualistic situations do not have the opportunity for such a process, and their productivity, quality of decision making, and achievement therefore suffer.

Public advocacy and commitment

Promotive interaction includes advocating that cooperators increase their efforts to accomplish the group's goals and publicly committing oneself to do the same. Commitment can be defined as the binding or pledging of the individual to an act or decision. To the extent that people act in the absence of coercion, commit themselves in front of others to act, or invest time, money, or personal prestige in an activity, they come to see themselves as believers in that sort of activity and develop a personal interest in it. Individuals become more committed to attitudes that are made public than to attitudes that remain private. People are particularly prone to increase their commitment to actions that they have attempted to persuade another to adopt.

Mutual influence

During the exchange of information, individuals share ideas and information and use each other's resources to maximize their productivity and achievement. This process entails mutual influence in which cooperators consider each other's ideas and conclusions and coordinate their efforts. Participants must be open to influence attempts aimed at facilitating the accomplishment of shared goals, must trust each other *not* to use the resources being shared in detrimental ways, and must form emotional bonds that result in commitment to each other's welfare and success. Influence can be exerted in three ways within social situations: direct influence, social modeling, and situational norms. Students will be receptive to others' attempts to influence them directly to the extent that they perceive a cooperative relationship among goals attained. In cooperative situations, students benefit from the group's modeling effective and committed behaviors, skills, and attitudes. Visible and credible models who demonstrate the recommended attitudes and behaviors and who directly discuss their importance are powerful influences. Finally, achievement is influenced by whether or not the group's norms favor high performance. In cooperative situations, everyone benefits from the efforts of cooperators. Because it is in each student's best interests to encourage the productivity of collaborators, the group's norms support efforts to achieve. Furthermore, evidence suggests that in the generally competitive climate of most schools, success at academic tasks has little value for many individuals and could even be a deterrent to popularity with peers (Johnson and Johnson 1989a).

Motivation to achieve

Achievement is a we *thing, not a* me *thing, always the product of many heads and hands.*
                                                          —J.W. Atkinson

Motivation to achieve is reflected in the effort individuals commit to strive to acquire increased understanding and skills they perceive as meaningful and worthwhile. While humans might be born with a motivation to increase their competencies, motivation to achieve is basically induced through interpersonal processes, either internalized relationships or current interaction patterns within a learning situation. Depending on whether students interact within a context of positive, negative, or no interdependence, different patterns of interaction result, causing different motivational systems, which in turn affect achievement differently, determining expectations for future achievement. The motivational system promoted in cooperative situations includes intrinsic motivation, high expectations for success, high incentive to achieve based on mutual benefit, high epistemic curiosity and continuing interest in achievement, high commitment to achieve, and high persistence. The motivational system promoted in competitive situations includes extrinsic motivation to win, low expectations for success by all but those with the highest ability, low incentive to learn based on differential benefit, low epistemic curiosity, a lack of continuing interest to achieve, a lack of commitment to achieving, and low task persistence by most individuals. The motivational system promoted in individualistic situations includes extrinsic motivation to meet preset criteria of excellence, low expectations for success by all but those with the highest ability, an incentive to achieve based on self-benefit, low epistemic curiosity and continuing interest to achieve, low commitment to achieving, and low task persistence by most individuals.

Motivation is most commonly viewed as a combination of the perceived likelihood of success and the perceived incentive for success. The greater the likelihood of success and the more important it is to succeed, the higher the motivation. Success that is intrinsically rewarding is usually seen as more

desirable for learning than is having students believe that only extrinsic rewards are worthwhile. The likelihood of success is perceived as greater, and success is viewed as more important in cooperative than in competitive or individualistic learning situations (Johnson and Johnson 1989a). Striving for mutual benefit results in an emotional bonding, with collaborators liking each other, wanting to help each other succeed, and being committed to each other's well-being. These positive feelings toward the group and the other members could have a number of important influences on intrinsic motivation to achieve and actual productivity. In many cases, the relationships among group members can become more important than the actual rewards given for the work being done. Consequences provided by group members (for example, respect, liking, blame, rejection) can supplement or replace those produced by task performance (for example, salary or grades). Such consequences might be important in sustaining behavior during periods when no task-based reinforcement is received.

Interpersonal trust

To disclose one's reasoning and information, one must trust the other individuals involved in the situation to listen with respect. Trust is a central dynamic of promotive interaction. It tends to be developed and maintained in cooperative situations and tends to be absent and destroyed in competitive and individualistic situations (Deutsch 1958, 1960, 1962; Johnson 1971, 1973, 1974; Johnson and Noonan 1972). Trust includes several elements:

1. Anticipation of beneficial or harmful consequences (risk);
2. Realization that others have the power to determine the consequences of one's actions;
3. Expectation that the harmful consequences are more serious than the beneficial consequences;
4. Confidence that the others will behave in ways that ensure beneficial consequences for oneself (Deutsch 1962).

Interpersonal trust is built by placing one's consequences in the control of others and having one's confidence in the others confirmed. It is destroyed by placing one's consequences in the hands of others and having one's confidence in the others disconfirmed through their behaving in ways that ensure harmful consequences for oneself. Thus, trust includes two sets of behaviors. *Trusting* behavior is the willingness to risk beneficial or harmful consequences by making oneself vulnerable to another person. *Trustworthy* behavior is the willingness to respond to another person's taking risks in a way that ensures that the other person will experience beneficial consequences. To establish trust, two or more people must be trustworthy and trusting. In cooperative situations, individuals tend to be both trusting and trustworthy; in competitive situations, they tend to be distrusting and untrustworthy, using information to promote their own success and the other's failure.

Anxiety and performance
Cooperation typically produces less anxiety and stress and more effective coping strategies to deal with anxiety than does competition. Anxiety is one of the most pervasive barriers to productivity and positive interpersonal relationships, generally leading to an egocentric preoccupation with oneself, disruption of cognitive reasoning, and avoidance of the situation one fears. They in turn can mean skipping school or work, cutting classes or taking long breaks, or avoiding challenging situations at school or work. Furthermore, continued experience involving even moderate levels of anxiety over a number of years can produce psychological and physiological harm. Especially for individuals with a chronic high state of anxiety, cooperation promotes a better climate for learning and work.

Summary of promotive interaction
Positive interdependence results in promotive interaction, which in turn promotes efforts to achieve, positive interpersonal relationships, and psychological health. Promotive interaction can be defined as individuals encouraging and facilitating each other's efforts to achieve, complete tasks, and produce to reach the group's goals. It is characterized by individuals providing each other with efficient and effective assistance, exchanging needed resources, such as information and materials, and processing information more efficiently and effectively, providing each other with feedback to improve their subsequent performance of their assigned tasks and responsibilities, challenging each other's conclusions and reasoning to promote higher-quality decision making and greater

insight into the problems being considered, advocating the exertion of effort to achieve mutual goals, influencing each other's efforts to achieve the group's goals, being motivated to strive for mutual benefit, acting in trusting and trustworthy ways, and exhibiting a moderate level of arousal characterized by low anxiety and stress. Oppositional interaction results in the opposite pattern of interaction. Promotive interaction results in a number of important outcomes that can be subsumed under three broad categories: effort exerted to achieve, quality of relationships among participants, and participants' psychological adjustment and social competence.

Learning Outcomes

Different learning outcomes result from the interaction between students promoted by the use of cooperative, competitive, and individualistic goal structures (Johnson and Johnson 1989a). The numerous outcomes of cooperative efforts can be subsumed under the three broad categories cited in the previous paragraph. Because research participants have varied as to economic class, age, sex, and cultural background, because a wide variety of research tasks and measures of the dependent variables have been used, and because the research has been conducted by many different researchers with markedly different orientations working in different settings and in different decades, the overall body of research on social interdependence has considerable generalizability.

Effort to achieve

Achievement. Over 375 studies have been conducted over the past 90 years to answer the question of how successful competitive, individualistic, and cooperative efforts are in promoting productivity and achievement (see table 3) (Johnson and Johnson 1989a). When all of the studies were included in the analysis, the average student cooperating performed at about two-thirds a standard deviation above the average student learning within a competitive (effect size = 0.67) or individualistic (effect size = 0.64) situation. When only high-quality studies were included in the analysis, the effect sizes were 0.88 and 0.61, respectively. When only the college and adult studies were included in the analysis, the results were similar. Cooperative learning promoted higher achievement than did competitive or individualistic learning (effect sizes = 0.59 and 0.62, respectively). Interestingly, com-

TABLE 3

SOCIAL INTERDEPENDENCE: Weighted Findings

Achievement

	Mean	Standard Deviation	Number
Total Studies			
Cooperative versus competitive	0.67	0.93	129
Cooperative versus individualistic	0.64	0.79	184
Competitive versus individualistic	0.30	0.77	38
High-Quality Studies			
Cooperative versus competitive	0.88	1.13	51
Cooperative versus individualistic	0.61	0.63	104
Competitive versus individualistic	0.07	0.61	24
Mixed Operationalization			
Cooperative versus competitive	0.40	0.62	23
Cooperative versus individualistic	0.42	0.65	12
Pure Operationalization			
Cooperative versus competitive	0.71	1.01	96
Cooperative versus individualistic	0.65	0.81	164
College and Adult			
Cooperative versus competitive	0.59	0.86	52
Cooperative versus individualistic	0.62	0.90	96
Competitive versus individualistic	0.67	0.90	17

petition promoted higher achievement than did individualistic learning (effect size = 0.67). Cooperative learning, furthermore, resulted in more higher-level reasoning, more frequent generation of new ideas and solutions (i.e., process gain), and greater transfer of what is learned within one situation to another (i.e., group to individual transfer) than did competitive or individualistic learning.

Some cooperative learning procedures contained a mixture of cooperative, competitive, and individualistic efforts; others were "pure." The original jigsaw procedure (Aronson et al. 1978), for example, is a combination of resource interdependence (cooperative) and individual reward structure (individualistic). Teams-games-tournaments (DeVries and Edwards 1974) and student-teams-achievement-divisions (Slavin 1980) are mixtures of cooperation and intergroup competition. Team-Assisted Instruction (Slavin, Leavey, and Madden 1982) is a mixture of individualistic and cooperative learning. When the results of "pure" and "mixed" cooperative learning were compared, "pure" produced higher achievement (cooperative versus competitive, pure = 0.71 and mixed = 0.40, cooperative versus individualistic, pure = 0.65 and mixed = 0.42).

The potential value of cooperative learning in large college classes is highlighted by a recent study designed to identify what specific factors contributed to students' learning in large classes (Wulff, Nyquist, and Abbott 1987). The survey of 800 college students found that the second most frequently cited factor contributing to their learning in large classes was "other students," leading the researchers to conclude that faculty might wish to use cooperative learning in large classes (p. 29). A comparison of the cost-effectiveness of four academic strategies concluded that working with classmates is the most cost-effective support system for increasing college students' achievement (Levin, Glass, and Meister 1984).

That working together to achieve a common goal results in higher achievement and greater productivity than does working alone is so well confirmed by so much research that it stands as one of the strongest principles of social and organizational psychology. Cooperative learning is indicated whenever the goals of learning are highly important, mastery and retention are important, the task is complex or conceptual, problem solving is desired, divergent thinking or creativity is desired, quality of performance is expected, and higher-level reasoning strategies and critical thinking are needed.

Why does cooperation result in higher achievement? The critical issue in understanding the relationship between cooperation and achievement is specifying the variables that mediate the relationship. Simply placing students in groups and telling them to work together does not of itself promote higher achievement. It is only under certain conditions that the group's efforts can be expected to be more productive than individual efforts. Those conditions are clearly perceived positive interdependence, considerable promotive (face-to-face) interaction, felt personal responsibility (individual accountability) to achieve the group's goals, frequent use of relevant interpersonal and small-group skills, and periodic and regular group processing (Johnson and Johnson 1989a).

Critical thinking competencies. In many subject areas, teaching facts and theories is considered secondary to the development of students' critical thinking and use of higher-level reasoning. The aim of science education, for example, has been to develop individuals who can sort sense from nonsense or who have the abilities involved in critical thinking of grasping information, examining it, evaluating it for soundness, and applying it appropriately. The application, evaluation, and synthesis of knowledge and other higher-level reasoning skills, however, are often neglected in college classes. Cooperative learning promotes a greater use of higher-level reasoning strategies and critical thinking than competitive or individualistic learning strategies (Gabbert, Johnson, and Johnson 1986; Johnson and Johnson 1981; Johnson, Skon, and Johnson 1980; Skon, Johnson, and Johnson 1981). Cooperative learning experiences, for example, promote more frequent insight into and use of higher-level cognitive and moral reasoning strategies than do competitive or individualistic learning experiences (effect sizes = 0.93 and 0.97, respectively).

Simply placing students in groups and telling them to work together does not of itself promote higher achievement.

In addition to the research directly relating cooperative learning with critical thinking, certain lines of research link critical thinking and cooperative learning. At least three elements of teaching make a difference in college students' gains in thinking skills: (1) discussion among students, (2) explicit emphasis on problem-solving procedures and methods using varied examples, and (3) verbalization of methods and strategies to encourage development of metacognition (McKeachie 1988).

> *Student participation, teacher encouragement, and student-to-student interaction positively relate to improved critical thinking. These three activities confirm other research and theory stressing the importance of active practice, motivation, and feedback in thinking skills as well as other skills. This confirms that discussions, especially in small classes, are superior to lectures in improving thinking and problem solving* (p. 1).

The explicit teaching of higher-level reasoning and critical thinking does not depend on what is taught, but rather on *how* it is taught (Ruggiero 1988). "The only significant change that is required is a change in teaching methodology" (p. 12). Cooperative learning is such a change.

Research indicates that cooperative learning is an important procedure for involving students in meaningful activities in the classroom and engaging in situated cognition (Brown, Collins, and Duguid 1989; Lave 1988; Schoenfeld 1985, 1989). Higher-level writing assignments can also best be done by cooperative peer response groups (DiPardo and Freedman 1988).

Attitudes toward subject area. Cooperative learning experiences, compared with competitive and individualistic ones, promote more positive attitudes toward the subject area, more positive attitudes toward the instructional experience, and more continuing motivation to learn more about the subject area being studied (Johnson and Johnson 1989a). A study comparing group discussion and lecturing found that students in discussion sections had significantly more favorable attitudes toward psychology than the other groups; a follow-up of the students three years later revealed that seven students each from the tutorial and discussion groups majored in psychology, whereas none of those in the recitation group did so (Guetzkow, Kelly, and McKeachie 1954; McKeachie 1951). Students who had opportunities in class to interact with classmates and the instructor were more satisfied with their learning experience than students who were taught exclusively by lecture (Bligh 1972). Students who participated in discussion groups in class were more likely to develop positive attitudes toward the course's subject matter (Kulik and Kulik 1979). And one of the major conclusions of the Harvard Assessment Seminars was that the use of cooperative learning groups resulted in a large increase in satisfaction with the class (Light 1990). These findings have important implications for influencing female and minority students to enter careers oriented toward science and mathematics.

Interpersonal relationships
Interpersonal attraction and cohesion. Cooperative learning experiences, compared with competitive and individualistic ones and "traditional instruction," promote considerably more liking among students (effect sizes = 0.67 and 0.60, respectively) (Johnson and Johnson 1989a; Johnson, Johnson, and Maruyama 1983), regardless of individual differences in ability, sex, handicapping conditions, ethnic mem-

bership, social class, or task orientation (see table 4). Students who studied cooperatively, compared with those who studied competitively or individualistically, developed considerably more commitment and caring for each other, no matter what their initial impressions of and attitudes toward each other. When only the high-quality studies were included in the analysis, the effect sizes were 0.82 (cooperative versus competitive) and 0.62 (cooperative versus individualistic), respectively. The effect sizes were higher for the studies using pure operationalizations of cooperative learning than for studies using mixed operationalizations (cooperative versus competitive, pure = 0.79 and mixed = 0.46; cooperative versus individualistic, pure = 0.66 and mixed = 0.36). Students learning cooperatively also liked the instructor better and perceived the instructor as being more supportive and accepting academically and personally. For the college and adult studies, cooperative experiences resulted in greater interpersonal attraction than did competitive or individualistic experiences (effect sizes = 0.83 and 0.40, respectively). Competition promoted greater interpersonal attraction than did individualistic efforts (effect size = 0.84).

To be productive, a class of students must cohere and share a positive emotional climate. As relationships within the class or college become more positive, absenteeism decreases and students' commitment to learning, feeling of personal responsibility to complete the assigned work, willingness to take on difficult tasks, motivation and persistence in working on tasks, satisfaction and morale, willingness to endure pain and frustration to succeed, willingness to defend the college against external criticism or attack, willingness to listen to and be influenced by peers, commitment to peers' success and growth, and productivity and achievement can be expected to increase (Johnson and F. Johnson 1991; Johnson and Johnson 1989a; Watson and Johnson 1972).

In addition, when a class includes students who are different with regard to ethnicity, social class, language, and ability, cooperative learning experiences are a necessity for building positive peer relationships—especially for contemporary colleges, which are now witnessing an increasing number of international students on campus (Scully 1981) and an increasing number of African-American students attending predominantly white colleges (National Center for Educational Statistics 1984). Studies on desegregation indicate that

TABLE 4

SOCIAL INTERDEPENDENCE: Weighted Findings

Interpersonal Attraction

	Mean	Standard Deviation	Number
Total Studies			
Cooperative versus competitive	0.67	0.49	93
Cooperative versus individualistic	0.60	0.58	60
Competitive versus individualistic	0.08	0.70	15
High-Quality Studies			
Cooperative versus competitive	0.82	0.40	37
Cooperative versus individualistic	0.62	0.53	44
Competitive versus individualistic	0.27	0.60	11
Mixed Operationalization			
Cooperative versus competitive	0.46	0.29	37
Cooperative versus individualistic	0.36	0.45	10
Pure Operationalization			
Cooperative versus competitive	0.79	0.56	54
Cooperative versus individualistic	0.66	0.60	49
College and Adult			
Cooperative versus competitive	0.83	0.47	34
Cooperative versus individualistic	0.40	0.73	15
Competitive versus individualistic	0.84	0.21	2

cooperation promoted more positive cross-ethnic relationships than competitive (effect size = 0.54) or individualistic (effect size = 0.44) learning experiences (Johnson and Johnson 1989a). Cross-handicapped relationships were also more positive in cooperative than in competitive (effect size = 0.70) or individualistic (effect size = 0.64) learning experiences.

Social support. Table 5 indicates that cooperation resulted in greater social support than did competitive or individualistic efforts (effect sizes = 0.62 and 0.70, respectively). For the high-quality studies, the results were comparable (effect sizes = 0.83 and 0.72, respectively). The pure operationali-

TABLE 5

SOCIAL INTERDEPENDENCE: Weighted Findings

Social Support

	Mean	Standard Deviation	Number
Total Studies			
Cooperative versus competitive	0.62	0.44	84
Cooperative versus individualistic	0.70	0.45	72
Competitive versus individualistic	-0.13	0.36	19
High-Quality Studies			
Cooperative versus competitive	0.83	0.46	41
Cooperative versus individualistic	0.72	0.47	62
Competitive versus individualistic	-0.13	0.36	19
Mixed Operationalization			
Cooperative versus competitive	0.45	0.23	16
Cooperative versus individualistic	0.02	0.35	6
Pure Operationalization			
Cooperative versus competitive	0.73	0.46	58
Cooperative versus individualistic	0.77	0.40	65
College and Adult			
Cooperative versus competitive	0.70	0.58	29
Cooperative versus individualistic	0.36	0.37	16
Competitive versus individualistic	-0.45	0.25	5

zations of cooperation promoted greater social support (compared with competition) than did the mixed operationalizations (effect sizes = 0.73 and 0.45, respectively). When cooperative and individualistic learning experiences were compared, the results were even more extreme (effect sizes = 0.77 and 0.02, respectively). When only the college and adult samples were included, the effect sizes were 0.70 and 0.36. Competitive experiences promoted less social support than did individualistic experiences (effect size = -0.45).

Social support tends to be related to several factors:

1. Achievement, successful problem solving, persistence on challenging tasks under frustrating conditions, lack of cog-

nitive interference during problem solving, lack of absenteeism, academic and career aspirations, more appropriate
seeking of assistance, retention, job satisfaction, high
morale, and greater compliance with regimens and behavioral patterns that increase health and productivity;
2. A longer life, recovering from illness and injury faster and
more completely, and experiencing less severe illnesses;
3. Psychological health and adjustment, lack of neuroticism
and psychopathology, reduction of psychological distress,
the ability to cope effectively with stressful situations, self-
reliance and autonomy, a coherent and integrated self-
identity, greater psychological safety, higher self-esteem,
increased general happiness, and increased interpersonal
skills;
4. Effective management of stress by providing the caring,
information, resources, and feedback individuals need
to cope with stress, reducing the number and severity of
stressful events in an individual's life, reducing anxiety,
and helping to appraise the nature of the stress and one's
ability to deal with it constructively; and
5. The emotional support and encouragement individuals
need to cope with the risk that is inherently involved in
challenging one's competence in striving to grow and
develop (Johnson and Johnson 1989a).

The importance of social support has been ignored in education over the past 30 years. The pressure to achieve should
always be matched with an equal level of social support; that
is, challenge and security must be kept in balance (Pelz and
Andrews 1976). Whenever increased demands and pressure
to be productive are placed on students (and faculty), social
support should be increased correspondingly.

Student retention. According to the Study Group on the
Conditions of Excellence in Higher Education:

*Traditional classroom teaching practices in higher education
favor the assertive student. But our analysis indicates that
instructors should give greater attention to the passive or
reticent student. . . . Passivity is an important warning sign
that may reflect a lack of involvement that impedes the
learning process and leads to unnecessary attrition*
(National Institute of Education 1984, p. 23).

Approximately one-half of all students who leave college do so during their freshman year (Terenzini 1986), and many of the departures take place during the first semester (Blanc, Debuhr, and Martin 1983). The major reasons for dropping out of college could be failure to establish a social network of friends and classmates and to become academically involved in classes.

The greater the degree of students' involvement in their college learning experience, the more likely they are to persist to graduation (Tinto 1975, 1987). The processes of social involvement, integration, and bonding with classmates are strongly related to higher rates of retention. On the basis of research conducted over 10 years, students' involvement academically and socially in college is the cornerstone of persistence and achievement (Astin 1985), and active involvement in learning is especially critical for "withdrawal-prone" students, such as disadvantaged minorities, who have been found to be particularly passive in academic settings (Astin et al. 1972).

Cooperative learning experiences tend to lower attrition rates in college. In one study, students working on open-ended problems in small groups of four to seven were more likely to display lower rates of attrition and higher rates of academic achievement than those not involved in group learning (Wales and Stager 1978). The five-year retention rate for African-American students majoring in math or science at Berkeley who were involved in cooperative learning, for example, was 65 percent, compared to 41 percent for African-American students not involved (Treisman 1985). The percentage of African-American students involved in cooperative learning who graduated in mathematics-based majors was 44 percent, compared to only 10 percent for a control group of African-American students not participating in cooperative learning groups.

College students report greater satisfaction with courses that allow them to engage in group discussion (Bligh 1972; Kulik and Kulik 1979), and students are more likely to stay in college if they are satisfied with the learning experience (Noel 1985). Cooperative learning allows for significant amounts of meaningful discussion, enhancing students' satisfaction with the learning experience and promoting retention.

Faculty relationships with students. Many college faculty report that they get to know their students better when they use cooperative learning groups. The process of observing students work in small groups and then intervening seems to create more personal and informal interactions between the instructor and the students than do lectures and discussions involving the whole class. Interacting with students in small groups, for example, gives instructors a chance to learn and address students by name. "Addressing students by name" correlates significantly with students' overall satisfaction with the course and the instructor (Murray 1985). Such informal interactions also positively affect student retention (Astin 1977), for when faculty get to know students better in class, they could be more likely to interact with students informally outside the classroom. And the quantity and quality of out-of-class contact with faculty are strongly associated with students' retention (Pascarella 1980).

The importance of peer relationships. Peer relationships contribute to social and cognitive development and to socialization in numerous ways:

1. *In their interaction with peers, individuals directly learn attitudes, values, skills, and information unobtainable from adults.* In their interaction with each other, individuals imitate each other's behavior and identify with friends possessing admired competencies. Through providing models, reinforcement, and direct learning, peers shape a wide variety of social behaviors, attitudes, and perspectives.
2. *Interaction with peers provides support, opportunities, and models for prosocial behavior.* In one's interactions with peers, one helps, comforts, shares with, takes care of, assists, and gives to others. Without peers with whom to engage in such behaviors, many forms of prosocial values and commitments could not be developed. Conversely, whether or not individuals engage in problem or transitional behavior, such as the use of illegal drugs and delinquency, is related to the perceptions of their friends' attitudes toward such behaviors. Being rejected by one's peers tends to result in antisocial behavioral patterns characterized by aggressiveness, disruptiveness, and other negatively perceived behaviors.

3. *Peers provide models of, expectations of, directions for, and reinforcements of learning to control impulses.* Individuals frequently lack the perspective of time needed to tolerate delays in gratification. As they develop and are socialized, the focus on their own immediate impulses and needs is replaced with the ability to take longer perspectives of time. Peer interaction involving aggressive impulses like, for example, rough-and-tumble play promotes the acquisition of a repertoire of effective aggressive behaviors and helps establish the necessary regulatory mechanisms for modulating aggressive actions.
4. *Students learn to view situations and problems from perspectives other than their own.* Taking such perspectives is one of the most critical competencies for cognitive and social development. All psychological development can be described as a progressive loss of egocentrism and an increase in ability to take wider and more complex perspectives. It is primarily in interaction with peers that egocentrism is lost and the ability to take a wider perspective is gained.
5. *Relationships with peers are powerful influences on the development of the values and the social sensitivity required for autonomy.* Autonomy is the ability to understand what others expect in any given situation and to be free to choose whether to meet their expectations. Autonomous people are independent of both extreme inner- or outer-directedness. When making decisions about appropriate social behavior, autonomous people tend to consider both their internal values and the situation and then respond in flexible and appropriate ways. Autonomy is the result of the internalization of values (including appropriate self-approval) derived from caring and supportive relationships, and the acquisition of social skills and sensitivity. Individuals with a history of isolation from or rejection by peers often are inappropriately other-directed. They conform to group pressures even when they believe the recommended actions are wrong or inappropriate.
6. *Close and intimate relationships with peers provide others with whom young people can share their thoughts and feelings, aspirations and hopes, dreams and fantasies, joys and pains.* Young people need constructive peer relationships to avoid the pain of loneliness.

7. *Peer relationships help develop a frame of reference for perceiving oneself.* Throughout infancy, childhood, adolescence, and early adulthood, a person moves though several successive and overlapping identities. The physical changes involved in growth, increasing number of experiences with other people, increasing responsibilities, and general cognitive and social development all cause changes in self-definition. The final result should be a coherent and integrated identity. In peer relationships, children and adolescents become aware of the similarities and differences between themselves and others. They experiment with a variety of social roles that help them integrate their own sense of self. In peer relationships, values and attitudes are clarified and integrated into an individual's self-definition, gender typing and its impact on one's identity, for example.

8. *Coalitions formed during childhood and adolescence provide help and assistance throughout adulthood.*

9. *Friendships during childhood and adolescence seem to decrease the risk of mental disorder.* The ability to maintain independent, cooperative relationships is a prime manifestation of psychological health. Poor peer relationships in elementary school predict psychological disturbance and delinquency in high school, and poor peer relationships in high school predict adult pathology.

10. *In both educational and work settings, peers have a strong influence on productivity.* Greater achievement is typical in collaborative situations where peers work together than in situations where individuals work alone.

11. *Students' educational aspirations could be more influenced by peers than by any other social influence.* Similarly, ambition in career settings is greatly influenced by peers. In instructional settings, peer relationships can be structured to create meaningful interdependence through learning cooperatively with peers. In cooperative learning situations, students experience feelings of belonging, acceptance, support, and caring, and the social skills and social roles required for maintaining interdependent relationships can be taught and practiced (Johnson 1980; Johnson and Johnson 1989a).

Through repeated cooperative experiences, students can develop the social sensitivity to learn what behavior is expected from others and the actual skills and autonomy to meet such expectations if they so desire. Through holding each other accountable for appropriate social behavior, students can greatly influence the values they internalize and the self-control they develop. Through belonging to a series of inter-dependent relationships, students learn and internalize values. Through prolonged cooperative interaction with other people, healthy social development and general trust rather than dis-trust of other people, the ability to view situations and prob-lems from a variety of perspectives, a meaningful sense of direction and purpose in life, an awareness of mutual inter-dependence with others, and an integrated and coherent sense of personal identity take place (Johnson 1979; Johnson and Matross 1977).

For peer relationships to be constructive influences, they must promote feelings of belonging, acceptance, support, and caring rather than feelings of hostility and rejection (Johnson 1980). Being accepted by peers is related to willingness to engage in social interaction, using abilities to achieve goals, and providing positive social rewards for peers. Isolation from peers is associated with high anxiety, low self-esteem, poor interpersonal skills, emotional handicaps, and psychological pathology. Rejection by peers is related to disruptive class-room behavior, hostile behavior and negative affect, and neg-ative attitudes toward other students and school. To promote constructive influences from peers, teachers must therefore first ensure that students interact with each other and then that the interaction takes place within a cooperative context.

Psychological health
Psychological adjustment. When students leave college, they need the psychological health and stability required to build and maintain relationships in a career, family, and com-munity, to establish a basic and meaningful interdependence with other people, and to participate effectively in society. Studies on the relationship between cooperation and psycho-logical health indicate that cooperativeness is positively related to a number of indices of psychological health: emo-tional maturity, well-adjusted social relations, strong personal identity, and basic trust in and optimism about people (John-son and Johnson 1989a). Competitiveness seems also to be related to a number of indices of psychological health, while individualistic attitudes tend to be related to a number of in-

Being accepted by peers is related to willingness to engage in social interaction, using abilities to achieve goals, and providing positive social rewards for peers.

dices of psychological pathology: emotional immaturity, social maladjustment, delinquency, self-alienation, and self-rejection. Colleges and college classes should be organized cooperatively to reinforce those traits and tendencies that promote students' psychological well-being.

Accuracy of perspective. Taking a social perspective is the ability to understand how a situation appears to another person and how that person is reacting cognitively and emotionally to the situation. The opposite of taking a perspective is egocentrism, that is, being embedded in one's own viewpoint to the extent that one is unaware of other points of view and of the limitation of one's perspective. Cooperative learning tends to promote greater cognitive and affective perspective taking than do competitive or individualistic learning experiences (Johnson and Johnson 1989a). In one study, students participating in class discussions (as opposed to listening to lectures) showed greater insight (as rated by clinical psychologists) into problems of the young women depicted in the film, *The Feeling of Rejection* (Bovard 1951a, 1951b; McKeachie 1954).

Self-esteem. Table 6 indicates that cooperation tended to promote higher levels of self-esteem than did competitive and individualistic efforts (effect sizes = 0.58 and 0.44, respectively). When only the college and adult samples were included in the analyses, the results were similar for the comparison of cooperation and competition (effect size = 0.67) but lower for the comparison of cooperative and individualistic efforts (effect size = 0.19). Only one study compared the effects of competitive and individualistic efforts on self-esteem at the college level. High self-esteem seems desirable, because individuals with low self-esteem tend to:

1. Have low productivity because they set low goals for themselves, lack confidence in their ability, and assume that they will fail no matter how hard they try;
2. Be critical of others as well as themselves by looking for flaws in others and trying to tear them down;
3. Withdraw socially because they feel awkward, self-conscious, and vulnerable to rejection;
4. Be conforming, agreeable, highly persuadable, and highly influenced by criticism;

TABLE 6

SOCIAL INTERDEPENDENCE: Weighted Findings

Self-Esteem

	Mean	Standard Deviation	Number
Total Studies			
Cooperative versus competitive	0.58	0.56	56
Cooperative versus individualistic	0.44	0.40	38
Competitive versus individualistic	−0.23	0.42	19
High-Quality Studies			
Cooperative versus competitive	0.67	0.31	24
Cooperative versus individualistic	0.45	0.44	29
Competitive versus individualistic	−0.25	0.46	13
Mixed Operationalization			
Cooperative versus competitive	0.33	0.39	17
Cooperative versus individualistic	0.22	0.38	9
Pure Operationalization			
Cooperative versus competitive	0.74	0.59	36
Cooperative versus individualistic	0.51	0.40	27
College and Adult			
Cooperative versus competitive	0.67	0.93	18
Cooperative versus individualistic	0.19	0.47	5
Competitive versus individualistic	−0.46	0.00	1

5. Develop more psychological problems, such as anxiety, nervousness, insomnia, depression, and psychosomatic symptoms (Johnson and Johnson 1989a).

In competitive situations, self-esteem tends to be based on the contingent view of one's competence that "If I win, then I am worthwhile as a person, but if I lose, then I am not." Winners attribute their success to superior ability and attribute the failure of others to lack of ability, both of which contribute to self-aggrandizement. Losers, who are the vast majority, defensively tend to be self-disparaging and apprehensive about evaluation, and tend to withdraw psychologically and physically. In individualistic situations, students are isolated from one another, receive little direct comparison with or feedback from peers, and perceive evaluations as inaccurate and unrealistic. The result is a defensive avoidance, an apprehension of evaluation, and a distrust of peers. In cooperative situations, however, individuals tend to interact, promote each other's success, form multidimensional and realistic impressions of each other's competencies, and provide accurate feedback. Such interaction tends to promote a basic self-acceptance of oneself as a competent person.

Relationships among Outcomes

Bidirectional relationships exist among achievement, quality of interpersonal relationships, and psychological health (Johnson and Johnson 1989a), and each influences the others. The more students work cooperatively, the more they care about each other. Caring and committed friendships come from a sense of mutual accomplishment, from mutual pride in joint work, and from the bonding that results from joint efforts. And the more students care about each other, the harder they will work to achieve mutual goals for learning. Long-term and persistent efforts to achieve tend to come not from the head but from the heart (Johnson and Johnson 1989c). Individuals seek out opportunities to work with those they care about. As caring increases, so do feelings of personal responsibility to do one's share of the work, willingness to take on difficult tasks, motivation and persistence in working toward the goal, and willingness to endure pain and frustration on behalf of the group. All contribute to a group's productivity.

In addition, the joint success experienced in working together to get the job done enhances social competencies, self-esteem, and general psychological health. The healthier psychologically individuals are, the better able they are to work with others to achieve mutual goals. Joint efforts require coordination, effective communication, leadership, and management of conflicts. States of depression, anxiety, guilt, shame, and anger decrease the energy available to contribute to a cooperative effort.

Finally, the more positive interpersonal relationships are, the greater the psychological health of the individuals involved. Through the internalization of positive relationships, direct social support, shared intimacy, and expressions of caring, psychological health and the ability to cope with stress are built. The absence of caring and committed relationships and the presence of destructive relationships tend to increase psychological pathology. States of depression, anxiety, guilt, shame, and anger decrease individuals' ability to build and maintain caring and committed relationships. The healthier psychologically individuals are, the more meaningful and caring the relationships they can build and maintain.

Reducing the Discrepancy

With the amount of evidence available, it is surprising that the practice in college classrooms is so oriented toward competitive and individualistic learning and that colleges are so dominated by competitive and individualistic organizational structures. It is time for the discrepancy to be reduced between what research indicates is effective in teaching and what college faculty actually do. To do so, faculty must understand the role of the instructor in implementing cooperative learning. The next three sections focus on the instructor's role in using formal cooperative learning groups, informal cooperative learning groups, and cooperative base groups.

THE INSTRUCTOR'S ROLE IN COOPERATIVE LEARNING

Introduction to Formal Cooperative Learning Groups

Howard Eaton, an English professor at Douglas College in Vancouver, British Columbia, introduces his course, "Argumentative Writing for College Students," by stating to students:

> You have bought an opportunity to learn something, not a service. This is not a prison and it is not social entertainment of the useless and unemployable. This is work. Your tuition, furthermore, pays for only 15 percent of the cost for this course. The taxpayers fund the other 85 percent. You have, therefore, a social obligation that translates into two responsibilities: (1) You are responsible for your own learning. It is up to you to get something useful and interesting from this course; and (2) You are *equally* responsible for the learning of your groupmates. It is up to you to ensure that they get something useful and interesting from this course.

This introduction prepares students to do much of their work in formal cooperative learning groups.

Formal cooperative learning groups have fixed membership, usually last from a few days to a few weeks, and have a well-defined task to accomplish. The types of formal cooperative learning groups vary widely and include the jigsaw strategy, peer editing, checking homework, cooperative learning and testing, structured academic controversies, cooperative reading pairs, class presentations, laboratory groups, and drill-review pairs. Before exploring each type, this section describes the aspects of the instructor's role common to all.

The Instructor's Role

A favorite demonstration science lesson for elementary education students is to ask students to determine how long a candle burns in a quart jar. The instructor assigns students to groups of two, making the pairs as heterogeneous as possible. Each pair is given one candle and one quart jar (resource interdependence), the task of timing how long the candle will burn, and the cooperative goal of deciding on one answer that both members of the pair can explain. Students are to encourage each other's participation and relate what they are learning to previous lessons (social skills). Students light their candle, place the quart jar over it, and time how long the candle burns, and the answers from the pairs are announced. The instructor then gives the pairs the task of generating a number of answers to the question, "How many factors make a difference in how long the candle burns in the jar?" The answers from the pairs are written on the board. The pairs then repeat the experiment in ways that test which of the suggested factors do in fact make a difference in how long the candle burns. The next day, students individually take a quiz on the factors affecting the time a candle burns in a quart jar (individual accountability), and their scores are totaled to determine a joint score that, if high enough, earns them bonus points (reward interdependence). They spend some time discussing the helpful actions of each member and what they could do to be even more effective in the future (group processing).

Science experiments are only one of the many places cooperative learning can be used. Cooperative learning is appropriate for any instructional task. Whenever the learning goals are highly important, the task is complex or conceptual, problem solving is required, divergent thinking or creativity is desired, quality of performance is expected, higher-level reasoning strategies and critical thinking are needed, long-term retention is desired, or the social development of students is one of the major instructional goals, cooperative learning should be used (Johnson and Johnson 1989a).

In cooperative learning situations, the instructor forms the learning groups, teaches the basic concepts and strategies, monitors the functioning of the learning groups, intervenes to teach small-group skills, assists with the task when it is needed, evaluates students' learning using a criterion-referenced system, and ensures that the cooperative groups process how effectively members worked together. Students look to their peers for assistance, feedback, reinforcement, and support (see figure 2).

The instructor's role in using formal cooperative learning groups includes five parts:

1. Specifying the objectives for the lesson;
2. Making decisions about placing students in learning groups before the lesson is taught;
3. Explaining the task and goal structure to the students;
4. Monitoring the effectiveness of the cooperative learning groups and intervening to assist with tasks (such as an-

FIGURE 2

CHECKLIST FOR BETTER LEARNING GROUPS

I. Before the group begins:
    A. Expect them to learn, to enjoy, and to discover.
    B. Team up with people you don't know.
    C. Make your group heterogeneous.

II. As the group begins:
    A. Make a good first impression.
    B. Build the team.
       • Have a sociable, relaxed dinner together, without spouses or dates.
       • Do something that requires self-disclosure.
       • Take interpersonal risks that build trust.
       • Establish team goals.
    C. Plan ahead the data on group process that you need.
       • Harness computer skills for data analysis.
       • Examine and discuss the data for what it means about the group.

III. While the group is in existence:
    A. Work at increasing self-disclosure.
    B. Work at giving good feedback.
    C. Get the silent members involved.
    D. Confront the problems squarely and immediately.
       • Apply lessons from class work that address the problem.
       • Work on issues in the group even if they appear to be just between two members.
       • Don't assume you can't work with someone just because you don't like or respect them.
       • If the group can't solve a problem, consult the instructor as a group.
    E. Regularly review your data.
    F. Vary the leadership style needed.

IV. Wrapping up the group:
    A. Summarize and review your learning from group experiences.
       • Analyze the data to discover why the group was more effective or less so.
       • Provide final feedback to members on their behavior or contribution.
    B. Celebrate the group's accomplishments.
       • Have a dinner party with spouses/dates to help you celebrate.
       • Hold a final feedback meeting.
       • If it's hard to say "good-bye," do so nonverbally.

Source: Bowen and Jackson 1985–86

swering questions and teaching skills) or to increase students' interpersonal and group skills; and

5. Evaluating students' achievement and helping students discuss how well they collaborated with each other (Johnson and R. Johnson 1991; Johnson, Johnson, and Holubec 1990).

Specifying Instructional Objectives

An instructor needs to specify two types of objectives before the lesson begins. The *academic objective* must be specified at the correct level for the students and matched to the right level of instruction according to a conceptual or task analysis. The *social skills objective* details what interpersonal and small-group skills will be emphasized during the lesson. A common error many instructors make is to specify only academic objectives and to ignore the social skills objectives needed to train students to cooperate effectively with each other.

Decisions before Instruction Begins

Deciding on the size of the group

Once the objectives of the lesson are clear, the instructor must decide what size of learning group is optimal. Cooperative learning groups typically range from two to four individuals. The shorter the amount of time available, the smaller the group should be; the larger the group, the more resources available for the group's work but the more skills required to ensure that the group works productively. Sometimes the materials or equipment available or the specific nature of the task dictate the size of the group.

Assigning students to groups

Teachers often ask four basic questions about assigning students to groups:

1. *Should learning groups be homogeneous or heterogeneous in terms of members' ability?* At times, cooperative learning groups with homogeneous abilities can be used to master specific skills or to achieve certain instructional objectives. Generally, however, instructors should maximize the heterogeneity of students, placing high-, medium-, and low-achieving students in the same learning group. More elaborative thinking, more frequent giving and receiving of explanations, and greater perspective tak-

ing in discussing material seem to occur in heterogeneous groups, all of which increase the depth of understanding, the quality of reasoning, and the accuracy of long-term retention.

2. *Should non-task-oriented students be placed in learning groups with task-oriented peers or be separated?* To keep nonacademically oriented students on task, it often helps to place them in a cooperative learning group with task-oriented peers.

3. *Should students select whom they want to work with, or should the instructor assign students to groups?* Teacher-made groups often have the best mix because instructors can put together the best combinations of students. Random assignment, such as having students count off, is another possibility for achieving a good mix of students in each group. Having students select their own groups is often not very successful, because such groups often are homogeneous; for example, high-achieving students work with other high-achieving students, white students work with other white students, minority students work with other minority students, and males work with other males. Often less on-task behavior occurs in student-selected than in instructor-selected groups. A useful modification of having students select their own groups is to have students list whom they would like to work with and then place them in a learning group with one person they choose and the rest selected by the instructor.

4. *How long should the groups stay together?* This question has no simple answer. Some instructors keep cooperative learning groups together for an entire semester or year. Other instructors like to keep a learning group together only long enough to complete a task, unit, or chapter. Sooner or later, however, every student should work with every other classmate. The best advice is to allow groups to remain stable long enough for them to be successful. Breaking up groups that are having trouble functioning effectively is often counterproductive, because students do not learn the skills they need to resolve problems in collaborating with each other.

Arranging the room

How the instructor arranges the room is a symbolic message of what is appropriate behavior, and it can facilitate the learning groups in the classroom. Members of a learning group should sit close enough to each other to share materials, maintain eye contact with all group members, and talk to each other quietly without disrupting the other learning groups. The instructor should have clear access to every group. Students in each learning group need to be able to see all relevant task materials, see each other, converse with each other without raising their voices, and exchange ideas and materials in a comfortable atmosphere. The groups need to be far enough apart so that they do not interfere with each other's learning.

Planning instructional materials
To promote interdependence

Materials need to be distributed among group members so that all members participate and achieve. When a group is mature and experienced and group members have a high level of interpersonal and small-group skills, the instructor might not have to arrange materials in any specific way. When a group is new or when members are not very skilled, however, instructors might want to distribute materials in carefully planned ways to communicate that the assignment is to be a joint (not an individual) effort and that the students are in a learning situation where they sink or swim together. Three suggestions for doing so include:

1. *Materials interdependence.* Give only one copy of the materials to the group; students will then have to work together to be successful. This method is especially effective the first few times the group meets. After students are accustomed to working cooperatively, the instructor can give a copy of the materials to each student.

2. *Information interdependence.* Group members might each be given different books or resource materials to be synthesized. Or the materials could be arranged like a jigsaw puzzle so that each student has part of the materials needed to complete the task. Such procedures require that every member participate for the group to be successful.

3. *Interdependence from outside enemies.* Materials could be structured into a tournament format with competition between groups as the basis for promoting a perception of interdependence among group members (DeVries and

Edwards 1973). In the teams-games-tournament format, students are divided into heterogeneous cooperative learning teams to prepare members for a tournament in which they compete with the other teams. During the competition between groups, students individually compete against members of about the same ability from other teams. The team whose members do the best in the competition is pronounced the winner.

These procedures might not all be needed simultaneously. They are alternative methods of ensuring that students perceive that they are involved in a learning situation where they sink or swim together and behave collaboratively.

Assigning roles to ensure interdependence

Positive interdependence can also be structured through the assignment of complementary and interconnected roles to group members. In addition to their responsibility to learn, each group member can be assigned a responsibility to help group members work together effectively: a *summarizer* (who restates the group's major conclusions or answers), a *checker* (who ensures that all group members can explain how to arrive at an answer or conclusion), an *accuracy coach* (who corrects any mistakes in other members' explanations or summaries), an *elaborator* (who relates current concepts and strategies to material previously studied), a *researcher-runner* (who gets needed materials for the group and communicates with the other learning groups and the instructor), a *recorder* (who writes down the group's decisions and edits the group's report), an *encourager* (who ensures that all members contribute), and an *observer* (who keeps track of how well the group is cooperating). Assigning such roles is an effective method of teaching students social skills and fostering positive interdependence.

Roles like checking for understanding and elaborating are vital to high-quality learning but are often absent in college classrooms. The role of checker, for example, focuses on periodically asking each member of the group to explain what is being learned. "Checking for comprehension" is significantly associated with higher levels of students' learning and achievement (Rosenshine and Stevens 1986). A three-year study to improve teaching as part of a college faculty development program found that the teaching behavior faculty and

"Checking for comprehension" is significantly associated with higher levels of students' learning and achievement.

students perceived faculty to need the most help on was knowing whether the class understands the material or not and that checking for understanding is highly correlated with the instructor's overall effectiveness (Wilson 1987, p. 18). While the instructor cannot continually check the understanding of every student in the class (especially if the class has 300 students), the instructor can engineer such checking by having students work in cooperative groups and assigning one member the role of checker.

Structuring the Task and Positive Interdependence
Explaining the academic task
Instructors explain the academic task so that students are clear about the assignment and understand the objectives of the lesson. Direct teaching of concepts, principles, and strategies can occur at this point. Instructors might want to answer any questions students have about the concepts or facts they are to learn or apply in the lesson. Instructors need to consider several aspects of explaining an academic assignment to students:

1. *Set the task so that students are clear about the assignment.* Most instructors have considerable practice with this requirement already. Clear and specific instructions are crucial in warding off students' frustration. One advantage of cooperative learning groups is that they can handle more ambiguous tasks (when they are appropriate) than can students working alone. In cooperative learning groups, students who do not understand what they are to do ask group members for clarification before asking the instructor.
2. *Explain the objectives of the lesson and relate the concepts and information to be studied to students' past experience and learning to ensure maximum transfer and retention.* Explaining the intended outcomes of the lesson increases the likelihood that students will focus on the relevant concepts and information throughout the lesson.
3. *Define relevant concepts, explain procedures students should follow, and give examples to help students understand what they are to learn and do in completing the assignment.* To promote positive transfer of learning, point out the critical elements that separate this lesson from past learning.

4. *Ask the class specific questions to check students' under-standing of the assignment.* Such questioning ensures that thorough two-way communication ensues, that the assignment has been given effectively, and that students are ready to begin working on it.

Explaining criteria for success

Evaluation in cooperatively structured lessons must be criterion-referenced, and criteria must be established for acceptable work (rather than grading on a curve). Instructors could structure a second level of cooperation not only by keeping track of how well each group and its members perform, but also by setting criteria for the whole class to reach. Improvement (doing better this week than last week) could be set as a criterion of excellence.

Structuring positive interdependence

The instructor must communicate to students that they have a goal as a group and must work cooperatively. The importance of communicating to students that they will sink or swim together cannot be overemphasized. In a cooperative learning group, students are responsible for learning the assigned material, making sure that all other members of the group learn the assigned material, and making sure that all other class members successfully learn the assigned material, in that order. Instructors can do so in several ways:

1. *Structure positive goal interdependence by giving the group the responsibility of ensuring that all members achieve a prescribed level of mastery on the assigned materials.* Teachers might wish to say, "One answer from the group, everyone has to agree, and everyone has to be able to explain how to solve the problem or complete the assignment." They might establish the prescribed level of mastery as individual levels of performance that each group member must achieve for the group as a whole to be successful (the group's goal is for each member to demonstrate 90 percent mastery on a curriculum unit) or improved scores, with the group's goal to ensure that all members do better this week than they did last week.
2. *Structure positive reward interdependence by providing rewards for the group.* Bonus points could be added to all members' academic scores when everyone in the

group achieves a certain criterion, or bonus points could be given to each member when the total of all group members' scores is above a preset criterion of excellence.

Positive interdependence creates encouragement from peers and support for learning. Such positive peer pressure influences underachieving students to become academically involved. Members of cooperative learning groups should give two interrelated messages: "Do your work—we're counting on you!" and "How can I help you to do better?"

Structuring individual accountability
One purpose of a cooperative group is to make each member a stronger individual in his or her own right. It is usually accomplished by maximizing each member's learning. A group is not truly cooperative if some members are "slackers" and let others do all the work. To ensure that all members learn and that groups know which members to encourage and help, instructors need to assess frequently each group member's level of performance. Observing each group member's pattern of participation, giving practice tests, randomly selecting members to explain answers, having members edit each other's work, having students teach what they know to someone else, and having students use what they have learned on a different problem are ways to structure individual accountability.

Structuring cooperation among groups
The positive outcomes found in a cooperative learning group can be extended throughout a whole class by structuring cooperation among groups. Bonus points could be given if all members of a class reach a preset criterion of excellence. When a group finishes its work, the instructor should encourage the members to find other groups that are finished and compare and explain answers and strategies.

Specifying desired behaviors
The word "cooperation" has many different connotations and uses. Instructors need to define cooperation operationally by specifying the behaviors that are appropriate and desirable within the learning groups. Behaviors that are appropriate when a group is first formed include "stay with your group and do not wander around the room," "use quiet voices,"

"take turns," and "use each other's names." When groups begin to function effectively, expected behaviors can be expanded:

1. Have each member explain how to arrive at the answer;
2. Ask each member to relate what is being learned to previous information learned;
3. Check to make sure everyone in the group understands the material and agrees with the answers;
4. Encourage everyone to participate;
5. Listen accurately to what other group members are saying;
6. Do not change your mind unless you are logically persuaded (majority rule does not promote learning);
7. Criticize ideas, not people.

Instructors should not make the list of expected behaviors too long. One or two behaviors to emphasize for a few lessons is enough. Students need to know what behavior is appropriate and desirable within a cooperative learning group, but they should not be overloaded with information.

Monitoring and Intervening
Monitoring students' behavior
The instructor's job begins in earnest when the cooperative learning groups start working: It is no time to go get a cup of coffee or grade some papers. Much of the time in cooperative learning situations should be spent observing group members to obtain a "window" into students' minds to see what they do and do not understand, and to see what problems they are having in working together cooperatively. Through working cooperatively, students make hidden thinking processes overt and subject to observation and commentary. The instructor will be able to observe how students are constructing their understanding of the assigned material. (See Johnson and F. Johnson [1991] and Johnson, Johnson, and Holubec [1991a, 1991b] for a variety of observation instruments and procedures that can be used for these purposes.)

Assisting with tasks
When monitoring the groups as they work, instructors should clarify instructions, review important procedures and strategies for completing the assignment, answer questions, and teach skills related to the task as necessary. When discussing the

concepts and information to be learned, instructors should use the language or terms relevant to the learning. Instead of saying, "Yes, that's right," instructors should say something more specific to the assignment, such as, "Yes, that's one way to find the main idea of a paragraph." The use of more specific statements reinforces the desired learning and promotes positive transfer by helping students associate a term with their learning. One way to intervene is to interview a cooperative learning group by asking, "What are you doing?" "Why are you doing it?" and "How will it help you?"

Intervening to teach social skills

While monitoring the learning groups, instructors will also find students who do not have the necessary social skills and groups where problems in cooperating have arisen. In these cases, instructors should intervene to suggest more effective procedures for working together and more effective behaviors for students to engage in. They might also wish to intervene and reinforce particularly effective and skillful behaviors they have noticed. (See Johnson [1990, 1991] and Johnson and F. Johnson [1991] for a list of social skills required for productive group work and activities that can be used in teaching them.)

Instructors should not intervene any more than is absolutely necessary. Most instructors are geared to jumping in and solving problems for students to get them back on track. With a little patience, they would find that cooperative groups can often work their way through their own problems and find not only a solution, but also a method of solving similar problems in the future. Choosing when to intervene and when not to is part of the art of teaching. But even when intervening, instructors can turn the problem back to the group to solve. Many instructors intervene by having members set aside their task, pointing out the problem, and asking the group to create three possible solutions and to decide which solution they are going to try first.

Evaluating Learning and Processing Interaction

Providing closure to the lesson

At the end of the lesson, students should be able to summarize what they have learned and to understand where they will use it in future lessons. Instructors might wish to summarize the major points in the lesson, ask students to recall ideas or give samples, and answer any final questions students have.

Evaluating the quality and quantity Of students' learning

Tests should be given and papers and presentations graded. For cooperative learning to be successful, the learning of group members must be evaluated by a criterion-referenced system.

Processing how well the group functioned

An old rule of observation is that if you observe, you must process your observations with the group. Even if class time is limited, some time should be spent in small-group processing as members discuss how effectively they worked together and what could be improved. Instructors might also wish to spend some time giving the whole class feedback and having students share incidents that occurred in their groups.

Discussing the group's functioning is essential. A common teaching error is to provide too brief a time for students to process the quality of their cooperation. Students do not learn from experiences they do not reflect on. If the learning groups are to function better tomorrow than they did today, members must receive feedback, reflect on how their actions could be more effective, and plan how to be even more skillful during the next group session.

Cooperative Learning Structures

Any assignment in any subject area can be structured cooperatively. The instructor decides on the objectives of the lesson, makes a number of decisions about the size of the group and the materials required to conduct the lesson, explains to students the task and the goal to be reached cooperatively, monitors the groups as they work, intervenes when it is necessary, and then evaluates students' learning and ensures the groups process how effectively they are functioning.

Using cooperative learning is not easy, and it can take years to become an expert. Instructors are faced with pressure to teach like everyone else, to have students learn alone, and not to let students look at each other's papers. Students are not accustomed to working together and are likely to be competitively oriented. The instructor could start small, taking one topic or one class and using cooperative learning until feeling comfortable with it, and then expand into other topics or classes. To implement cooperative learning successfully, the instructor needs to teach students the interpersonal and small-group skills required to collaborate, to structure and orchestrate intellectual inquiry within learning groups, and to form collaborative relations with others. Implementing cooperative learning in the classroom is not easy, but it is worth the effort. Formal cooperative learning groups can be structured in the following ways in college classrooms.

The jigsaw strategy

When an instructor has information to communicate to students, an alternative to lecturing is a procedure for structuring cooperative learning groups called "jigsaw" (Aronson et al. 1978). The steps for structuring a jigsaw lesson are as follows:

1. *Cooperative groups.* Assign students to cooperative groups. Distribute a set of materials, divisible into the number of members of the group (two, three, or four parts), to each group. Give each member one part of the set.
2. *Preparation pairs.* Assign students the cooperative task of meeting with someone else in the class who is a member of another learning group and who has the same section of the material and complete two tasks: (1) learn and become an expert on their material, and (2) plan how to teach the material to the other members of their group.
3. *Practice pairs.* Assign students the cooperative task of meeting with someone else in the class who is a member of another group and who has learned the same material and share ideas as to how the material could best be taught. These "practice pairs" review what each plans to teach its group and how. The best ideas of both are incorporated into each student's presentation.
4. *Cooperative groups.* Assign students the cooperative tasks of teaching their area of expertise to the other group members and learning the material being taught by the other members.
5. *Evaluation.* Assess students' degree of mastery of all the material. Recognize or reward the groups whose members all reach the preset criterion of excellence.
6. *Processing.* Have the cooperative triads process briefly by identifying at least one action each member did to help

the other members learn and at least three actions that could be added to improve members' learning next time.

Peer editing: Cooperative learning in composition

Cooperative learning groups should be used whenever a paper or composition is assigned to be written. For example, students could be asked to hand in a paper revised on the basis of two reviews by members of their cooperative learning group—in other words, a process writing procedure requiring a cooperative group.

The cooperative goal is for all group members to verify that each member's composition is perfect according to the criteria set by the teacher. One of their scores for the composition is the total number of errors made by the pair (the number of errors in their composition plus the number of errors in their group's compositions). An individual score on the quality of the composition could also be given.

The procedure for writing the assigned paper is as follows:

1. Students are assigned to a cooperative group. Each student is responsible for writing the assigned paper.
2. Each member describes to the cooperative group what he or she is planning to write. Group members listen carefully, probe with a set of questions, and outline the proposed research paper. The written outline is given to the member. This procedure is repeated with every member of the group.
3. Students search individually for the material, sources, and references they need to write their papers, keeping an eye out for material useful to the other members of their group.
4. Group members work together to write each member's first paragraph to ensure that all members have a clear start on their papers.
5. Students write their compositions individually. Cooperative papers are allowed if they clearly reflect twice the work of an individual's paper (for example, if an individual's paper is 10 pages long, a paper written by a pair should be 20 pages long).
6. When the papers are completed, members of the group proofread each other's compositions, correcting capitalization, punctuation, spelling, use of language, use of topic

sentence, organization, and conceptualization, and suggesting how to improve other aspects of the paper.

7. Students rewrite their papers, using group members' suggestions for revisions.
8. Group members reread each other's papers and sign their names on each paper, indicating that they guarantee the paper's high quality.
9. Each student submits to the instructor a copy of the paper that is signed by all group members, a copy of the critical reviews by group members, and a thoughtful description of how the paper was revised according to the suggestions of the group.

The criterion for success is a well-written composition by each student. Depending on the instructor's objectives, the compositions can be evaluated for grammar, punctuation, organization, content, or other criteria. Students are evaluated in two ways: Does the paper meet the criteria for adequacy, and do the papers of the other members of their cooperative group meet the criteria for adequacy?

While the students work, the teacher monitors the pairs, intervening when appropriate to help students master the needed writing and cooperative skills. When the papers are completed, members of the cooperative group discuss how effectively they worked together (listing the specific actions they engaged in to help each other), plan what behaviors they will emphasize in the next peer-editing assignment, and thank each other for their help.

Checking homework

The task is for students to bring completed homework to class and ensure that they understand how to do it correctly. When students enter the classroom, they meet in their cooperative learning groups, which should be heterogeneous in math and reading ability. The cooperative goal is to ensure that all group members bring their completed homework to class and understand how to do it correctly. Three roles are assigned: the *explainer* (who explains step by step how the homework is correctly completed), the *checker* (who verifies that the explanation is accurate, encourages, and coaches others if needed), and the *runner* (who carries materials to and from the instructor's desk). The runner goes to the instructor's desk, picks up the group's folder, hands out any materials in the folder to the appropriate members, and records how much of the assignment each member completed. At the end of the assigned review time, members' homework is placed in the group's folder, and the runner returns it to the instructor's desk. The explainer reads the first part of the assignment and explains step by step how to complete it correctly. The other group members check for accuracy. The roles are rotated clockwise around the group so that each member does an equal amount of explaining. The group should concentrate on the parts of the assignments members do not understand.

The criterion for success is for all members of the group to complete the homework correctly and understand how to do it. To ensure individual accountability, instructors should give regular examinations and daily select group members at random to explain how to solve randomly selected problems from the homework.

A simpler alternative is to assign students to pairs. The teacher randomly picks questions from the homework assignment. One student explains step by step the correct answer, while the other student listens, checks for accuracy, and prompts the explainer if he or she does not know the answer. Roles are switched for each question.

Cooperative learning and testing
Whenever a test is given, cooperative learning groups can serve as bookends by preparing students to take the test and providing a setting in which students review the test. Two of the purposes of testing are to evaluate how much each student knows and to assess what students need to review. Using the following procedure results in achieving both purposes and students' learning the material they did not understand before the test. It also prevents arguments with students after the test about which answer is correct.

Preparing for a test. Instructors give students study questions on which the examination will be based and time in class to prepare for the examination. Each student meets in a cooperative group of four and works to understand how to answer each study question correctly.

Students should be assigned heterogeneously to cooperative groups in terms of performance on previous tests. The cooperative goal is to ensure that all members of the group know and understand the material on which they will be

The roles are rotated clockwise around the group so that each member does an equal amount of explaining.

tested. Two roles are assigned: the *explainer* (who explains step by step how to solve each study question) and the *checker* (who verifies that the explanation is accurate, encourages, and coaches others if needed). The explainer reads a question and explains step by step how to answer it correctly, while the other group members check for accuracy. The roles are rotated clockwise around the group after each problem. When group members disagree about any question, the page number and paragraph where the procedures required to attain the answer must be found. The criterion for success is for all members of the group to understand the material on which they will be tested. If all members of the group score over 90 percent on the test, each receives five bonus points. Individual accountability is established by having each student take the examination.

Reviewing a test. To review a test:

1. Each student takes the test individually and hands his or her answers to the teacher.
2. During the next class period, students are randomly assigned to groups of four, and each group is divided into two pairs. Each pair retakes the test. The cooperative goal is to have one answer for each question that both agree on and both can explain. They cannot proceed until they agree on the answer.
3. The groups of four meet. The cooperative goal is for all members of the group to understand the material covered by the test. Group members confer on each question, and, on any question for which the two pairs have different answers, they find the page number and paragraph in the textbook where the answer is explained. Each group is responsible for ensuring that all members understand the material they missed on the test. If necessary, members of the group assign review homework to each other.

The criterion for success is that all members of the group understand the material on which they were tested, especially the knowledge relevant to the questions they missed. Individual accountability is established by having students explain what they know to members of the group. The instructor then randomly selects students to answer questions they missed on the test.

Structured academic controversies

Students in cooperative groups often disagree about what answers to assignments should be and how the group should function to maximize members' learning. Conflict is an inherent part of learning as old conclusions and concepts are challenged and modified to take into account new information and broader perspectives. Controversy is a type of academic conflict that exists when one student's ideas, information, conclusions, theories, and opinions are incompatible with those of another and the two seek to agree. When students become experienced in working cooperatively and when instructors wish to increase students' emotional involvement in learning and motivation to achieve, instructors can structure controversy into cooperative learning groups by following these five phases:

1. *Students are given the cooperative assignment* of discussing a designated topic and writing a group report in which they summarize what they have learned and recommend the procedures they think are best for solving the problem. Students are randomly assigned to groups of four, ensuring that both male and female and high-, medium-, and low-achieving students are all in the same group. The group is divided into two pairs; one pair is assigned the "pro" position, the other the "con" position on an issue being studied. Each pair prepares its position based on a packet of articles, stories, or information that supports the position. During the first class period, each pair develops its position and plans how to present the best case possible to the other pair. Near the end of the period, pairs are encouraged to compare notes with pairs from other groups who represent the same position.
2. *Each pair presents its position to the other pair,* with each member of the pair participating in the presentation equally. Members of the opposing pair are encouraged to listen carefully and take notes.
3. *The group discusses the issue following a set of rules* to help them criticize ideas without criticizing people, differentiate the two positions, and assess the degree of evidence and logic supporting each position.
4. *Pairs reverse perspectives* and argue the opposing position.
5. *Students drop their advocacy positions, clarify their understanding of each other's information and rationale, and*

begin work on their group's report. Groups of four reach a decision and come to a consensus on a position that is supported by facts and logic and can be defended by each member of the group. The report is evaluated on the basis of the quality of the writing, the evaluation of opinion and evidence, and the oral presentation of the report to the class. The students then take an individual test, and, if every member of the group achieves up to the criterion, they all receive bonus points. Finally, during the sixth class period, each group makes a 10-minute presentation to the entire class summarizing its report. All four members of the group are required to participate orally in the presentation (Johnson and Johnson 1987; Johnson, Johnson, and Smith 1986).

Positive interdependence is structured by having each group arrive at a consensus, submit one written report, and make one presentation; by jigsawing the materials to the pairs within the group; and by giving bonus points to members if all members learn the basic information contained in the two positions and score well on the test. Individual accountability is structured by asking each member of the pair to participate orally in the presentation of the position and, in the reversal of perspective, having each member of the group participate orally in the group's presentation, and by having each member take an individual test on the material. The social skills emphasized are those involved in systematically advocating an intellectual position, evaluating and criticizing the position advocated by others, and synthesizing and consensual decision making. Numerous academic and social benefits are derived from participating in such structured controversies (Johnson and Johnson 1987; Johnson, Johnson, and Smith 1986).

Cooperative reading pairs
Cooperative reading is defined as an activity that "typically involves two or more students working together to improve their understanding and retention of text material" (Dansereau 1987, p. 614). This strategy for cooperative reading is called MURDER, based on setting the **m**ood to study (creating a supportive environment), reading for **u**nderstanding (marking important and difficult ideas), **r**ecalling the material without referring to the text, correcting recall and amplifying and

storing it so as to **d**igest the assigned material, **e**xpanding knowledge by self-inquiry, and **r**eviewing mistakes (learning from tests) (Dansereau 1985). The method is effective for college students learning procedural, technical, and narrative text while working in cooperative pairs. The roles of recaller and listener/facilitator are given to each student, acting as equal partners.

Class presentations

Students required to present material in class should be assigned to cooperative groups and each group required to prepare and conduct a group presentation. The task is to prepare and present an informative and interesting presentation. The cooperative goal is for all members to learn the material being presented and to gain experience in making presentations. The individual accountability is for all members to participate equally in the presentation. The reward interdependence can be either a group grade for the presentation or a grade for each student, based on his or her part of the presentation, with bonus points given if all members participate in an integrated (rather than sequential) way.

Laboratory groups

One of the most common ways to involve students actively in learning is the use of laboratory or experimental groups in which students use the scientific method to conduct an inquiry. Instructors direct and supervise students working in pairs, threes, or fours to investigate, prove, and formulate hypotheses. The task is to conduct the experiment or exercise; the cooperative goal is for each group to complete the project. Members sign off on the project to indicate that they have contributed their share of the work, agree with its content, and can present or explain it. When a variety of materials are used (such as microscopes, slides, and samples), each member of the group might be given the responsibility for one of the materials. If appropriate, each student should be assigned a specific role. Individual accountability can be structured by having each member of the group present the group's report to a member of another group, by observing the groups to verify that all members are participating actively, and by giving an individual test on the content covered by the project.

Drill-review pairs

This procedure was developed for math classes, but any class requiring drill and review can use the procedure. The task for drill-review pairs is to correctly solve the assigned problems. The cooperative goal is to ensure that both members understand the strategies and procedures required to solve the problems correctly. Two roles are assigned: the *explainer* (who explains step by step how to solve the problem), and the *checker* (who verifies that the explanation is accurate, encourages, and coaches if needed). The two roles are rotated after each problem. The procedure is to assign students to pairs, assign each pair to a foursome, and implement the following procedure:

1. Person A reads the problem and explains step by step the procedures and strategies required to solve it. Person B checks the accuracy of the solution and provides encouragement and coaching if needed.
2. Person B solves the second problem, describing step by step the procedures and strategies required to solve it. Person A checks the accuracy of the solution and provides encouragement and coaching if needed.
3. When two problems are completed, the pair checks their answers with another pair. If they do not agree, they resolve the problem until they reach a consensus about the answer. If they do agree, they thank each other and continue work in their pairs.
4. The procedure continues until all problems are completed.

Individual accountability is structured by randomly picking one member of randomly selected pairs to explain how to solve a randomly selected problem.

Conclusions

While the essence of cooperative learning is positive interdependence, other essential components include individual accountability (where every student is accountable for both learning the assigned material and helping other members of the group learn), face-to-face interaction among students (where students promote each other's success), students' appropriately using interpersonal and group skills, and students' processing how effectively their learning group has functioned. These five essential components of cooperation form the conceptual basis for constructing cooperative procedures. Research supports the propositions that cooperation results in greater effort to achieve, more positive interpersonal relationships, and greater psychological health and self-esteem than competitive or individualistic efforts. The next section covers the instructor's role in implementing *informal* cooperative learning groups.

THE COOPERATIVE LECTURE

Sage on the Stage, Or Guide on the Side?

Each class session, instructors must choose whether to be "a sage on the stage" or "a guide on the side." In doing so, they might remember that the challenge in college teaching is not covering the material for students, but *uncovering* it.

The obstacles to learning from a lecture were made painfully obvious during a recent workshop on cooperative learning for students and faculty in Norway. The instructor was convinced that a short lecture in the informal cooperative learning format on the latest research on learning would be effective. He asked a focus question at the start, lectured for about 12 minutes, and asked the participants to prepare a summary of the main points and formulate at least one question. When he asked for a summary, people did not know what to write. One student jokingly asked, "What did you say between 'Here's the research' and 'Your task is to create a summary'?" Several faculty members agreed, saying, "I didn't know what you were talking about. The concepts were somewhat new to me, you were enthusiastic and spoke slowly and clearly, but I really didn't understand what you were talking about."

After the break during discussion of participants' reactions, some faculty came to the instructor's defense, saying, "Well, it was a pretty good lecture. It was just kind of new to us." But then a student in the back said, "I understood a little at the beginning, but a lot of lectures are like this for me." And a student in the front said (with emphasis), "This is what it's like for me every day."

From the look on the faces of the faculty, they understood for the first time in a long time what it is like to be a student, trying to make sense out of lectures, not understanding, and being frustrated with not understanding. Perhaps the instructor should have followed Wilbert McKeachie's advice on lecturing: "I lecture only when I'm convinced it will do more good than harm."

This section discusses the lure of lecturing, details the problems and enemies of lecturing, and describes the use of informal cooperative learning groups to make students cognitively active during lectures.

The Lure of Lecturing

Our survey of teaching methods suggests that . . . if we want students to become more effective in meaningful learning

---

*and thinking, they need to spend more time in active, mean-
ingful learning and thinking—not just sitting and passively
receiving information* (McKeachie 1986, p. 77).

No logic or wisdom or willpower could prevail to stop the
ancient Greek sailors. Buffeted by the hardships of life at sea,
the voices came out of the mist to them like a mystical, ethe-
real love song with tempting and seductive promises of
ecstasy and delight. The voices and the song were irresistible.
The mariners helplessly turned their ships to follow the Sirens'
call with scarcely a second thought. Lured to their destruction,
the sailors crashed their ships on the waiting rocks and
drowned in the tossing waves, struggling with their last breath
to reach the source of that beckoning song.

Centuries later, the Sirens still call. Professors seem drawn
to lecturing, crashing their teaching on the rocks in response
to the seductive and tempting attractions of explicating knowledge to an adoring audience and teaching as they were taught.
The lecture came into prominence when it was assumed that
John Locke was correct and that the untrained mind is like
a blank sheet of paper waiting for the instructor to write on
it, and that students' minds are empty vessels into which
instructors pour their wisdom. Because of these and other
assumptions, faculty lecture. Moreover, faculty often think
of their job in terms of three principal activities:

1. *To impart knowledge,* that is, the faculty's job is to give
   and the student's job is to receive;
2. *To classify students,* that is, to decide who gets which
   grade;
3. *To sort students into categories,* that is, to decide who does
   and does not meet the requirements to be graduated, go
   on to graduate school, and get a good job.

Faculty often experience frustration with this model of
teaching and learning. Students might not learn what faculty
think they are teaching students. Students' performance on
exams or their questions could indicate that they do not
understand the material in the way or to the extent that faculty
would like them to. Furthermore, students often ask boring
questions like "Will it be on the final exam?" to determine
whether the material is important, when what matters is
whether professionals in practice regularly use the concept
or procedure.

Such questions quickly wear down professors, prompting them to ask whether a better way exists to teach students. Many faculty also question their role in "selecting and weeding," instead wanting to be part of a "development" process. James Duderstadt, president of the University of Michigan, notes that universities have focused on selection processes in recruiting students and faculty and have given little or no attention to developing human potential (Sheahan and White 1990). A challenge to the four traditional models of excellence in higher education—reputation, content, resources, outcome—advocates a talent-development model in which the development of student and faculty talent is primary (Astin 1985). Thus, recognition is growing that faculty should think of their jobs in terms of:

The lecture came into prominence when it was assumed that . . . students' minds are empty vessels into which instructors pour their wisdom.

1. Helping students construct their own knowledge, requiring that the instructor and students are actively engaged with one another in constructing knowledge and understanding; and
2. Developing students' competencies and talents. Colleges and universities must do more than selecting high-achieving students for admission and then serving as a holding ground for four years while they mature. Faculty must "add value" by developing students' potential and transforming them into more knowledgeable and committed individuals. A cultivating philosophy must replace a weeding out philosophy.

Cooperative learning provides an alternative to the empty vessel model of teaching and learning, encouraging the development of students' talent by providing a carefully structured approach to getting students actively involved in constructing their own knowledge. Getting students cognitively, physically, emotionally, and psychologically involved in learning is an important step in turning around the passive and impersonal character of many college classrooms.

What Is Lecturing?

The definition
A lecture is an extended presentation in which the instructor presents factual information in an organized and logically sequenced way. It typically results in long periods of unin-

terrupted teacher-centered expository discourse that relegates students to the role of passive spectators in the college classroom. Normally, lecturing includes the use of reference notes, an occasional use of visual aids to enhance the information being presented, and responses to students' questions as the lecture progresses or at its end. Occasionally, the instructor hands out materials to help students follow the lecture. The lecturer presents the material to be learned in more or less final form, answers questions, presents principles, and elaborates on the entire content of what is to be learned.

Lecturing is currently the most common method of presenting information in colleges and universities, and in secondary and elementary schools. It is particularly popular for teaching large introductory sections of courses in disciplines like psychology, chemistry, and mathematics. Even in training programs in business and industry, lecturing dominates. Some of the reasons for its popularity are that it can be adapted to different audiences and time frames and that it keeps the professor at the center of all communication and attention in the classroom.

The rationale for and pedagogy of lecturing are based on theories of the structure and organization of knowledge, the psychology of meaningful verbal learning, and ideas from cognitive psychology associated with the representation and acquisition of knowledge. "Knowledge structures" become a means for organizing information about topics, dividing information into various categories, and showing relationships among various categories of information (Bruner 1960). Meaning emerges from new information only if it is tied into existing cognitive structures, and instructors should therefore organize information for students, present it clearly and precisely, and anchor it into cognitive structures formed from prior learning (Ausubel 1963). Declarative knowledge is represented in interrelated propositions or unifying ideas, existing cognitive structures must be cued so that students bring them from long-term memory into working memory, and students must process new knowledge by coding it and then storing it in their long-term memory (Gagne 1985).

Appropriate use
The correct question is not whether lecturing is better or worse than other methods of teaching but the purposes for which lecturing is appropriate. Considerable research has

been carried out on lecturing. From the research directly evaluating lecturing (see Bligh 1972; Costin 1972; Eble 1983; McKeachie 1967; Verner and Dickinson 1967), it can be concluded that lecturing is appropriate when the purpose is to:

1. *Disseminate information.* Lecturing is appropriate when faculty want to communicate a large amount of material to many students in a short period of time or when they want to supplement curricular materials that need to be updated or elaborated, when material has to be organized and presented in a particular way, or when faculty want to introduce an area.
2. *Present material that is not available elsewhere.* Lecturing is appropriate when information is not available in a readily accessible source, the information is original, or the information is too complex for students to learn on their own.
3. *Expose students to content in a brief time that might take them much longer to locate on their own,* when faculty need to teach information that must be integrated from many sources and students do not have the time, resources, or skills to do so.
4. *Arouse students' interest in a subject.* When a lecture is presented by a highly authoritative person in an interesting way, students might be intrigued and want to find out more about the subject. Skillful delivery of a lecture includes maintaining eye contact, avoiding distracting behaviors, modulating voice pitch and volume, and using appropriate gestures. Achievement is higher when presentations are clear (Good and Grouws 1977; Smith and Land 1981), delivered with enthusiasm (Armento 1977), and delivered with appropriate gestures and movements (Rosenshine 1968).
5. *Teach students who are primarily auditory learners.*

Parts of a lecture
A lecture has three parts: the introduction, the body, and the conclusion. Proponents of lecturing advise, "Tell them what you are going to tell them, tell them, and then tell them what you told them." First is a description of the learning objectives in a way that alerts students to what is to be covered in the lecture, then a presentation of the material to be learned in small steps organized logically so it is easy to follow, then

an integrative review of the main points. More specifically, the introduction should:

1. Arouse students' interest by indicating the relevance of the lecture to their goals;
2. Provide motivational cues, such as telling students that the material to be covered is important, useful, and difficult, and will be included on a test;
3. Make the objectives of the lecture explicit and set expectations about what will be included;
4. Use "advance organizers" (that is, concepts given to students before the material to be learned that provide a stable cognitive structure in which the new knowledge can be subsumed [Ausubel 1963]) by telling students in advance how the lecture is organized. The use of advance organizers can be helpful when students have no relevant information to which they can relate the new learning and when relevant cognitive structures are present but the learner is not likely to recognize them as relevant. Advance organizers provide students with general learning sets that help cue them to key ideas and organize those ideas in relationship to one another. Announcing the topic as a title, summarizing the major points to be made in the lecture, and defining the terms they might not know give students a cognitive structure into which to fit the material being presented, thus improving their comprehension of the material, making it meaningful to them, and improving their ability to recall and apply what they hear;
5. Prompt awareness of students' relevant knowledge by asking questions about knowledge or experience related to the topic, giving and asking for examples, and asking questions to show how students' prior knowledge relates to the material covered in the lecture. Students' prior knowledge should be explicitly related to the topic of the lecture.

The body of the lecture should cover the content while providing a logical organization for the material being presented (see Bligh 1972 for examples of ways to organize lectures). The body's logical organization should be explicitly communicated to students.

The conclusion summarizes the major points. The instructor asks students to recall ideas or give examples and answers any questions.

Despite the popularity of lecturing, obstacles and problems are associated with its use.

Problems with lecturing

Much of the research on lecturing compares lecturing with group discussion. While the conditions under which lecturing is more successful than group discussion have not been identified, a number of problems with lecturing have been found.

First, students' attention to what the instructor is saying decreases as the lecture proceeds. Research in the 1960s by D.H. Lloyd at the University of Reading in Berkshire, England, found that students attending lectures followed the pattern of settling in for five minutes, readily assimilating material for five minutes, confusion and boredom with assimilation falling off rapidly and remaining low for the bulk of the lecture, and some revival of attention at the end of the lecture (Penner 1984). Concentration during lectures of medical students, who presumably are highly motivated, rose sharply, peaked 10 to 15 minutes after the lecture began, and then fell steadily thereafter (Stuart and Rutherford 1978). Another research study in the 1960s, which analyzed the percentage of content contained in students' notes at different time intervals through the lecture, found that students wrote notes on 41 percent of the content presented during the first 15 minutes, 25 percent presented during 30 minutes, and only 20 percent of what had been presented during 45 minutes (reported in Penner 1984).

Second, it takes an educated, intelligent person oriented toward auditory learning to benefit from listening to lectures. In general, very little of a lecture can be recalled except by listeners with above-average education and intelligence (Verner and Dickinson 1967). Even the best conditions, when intelligent, motivated people listen to a brilliant scholar talk about an interesting topic, can have serious problems.

After 18 minutes, one-third of the audience and 10 percent of the platform guests were fidgeting. At 35 minutes, everyone was inattentive; at 45 minutes, trance was more noticeable than fidgeting; and at 47 minutes, some were asleep and at least one was reading. A casual check 24 hours later revealed that the audience recalled only insignificant details, and [they] were generally wrong (Verner and Dickinson 1967, p. 90).

Third, lecturing tends to promote only lower-level learning of factual information. An extensive series of studies concluded that, while lecturing was as (but not more) effective as reading or other methods in transmitting information, lecturing was clearly less effective in promoting thinking or in changing attitudes (Bligh 1972). A survey of 58 studies conducted between 1928 and 1967 comparing various characteristics of lectures versus discussions found that lectures and discussions did not differ significantly on lower-level learning (such as learning facts and principles), but that discussion appeared superior in developing higher-level problem solving and positive attitudes toward the course (Costin 1972). A separation of studies on lecturing according to whether they focused on factual learning, higher-level reasoning, attitudes, or motivation found lectures to be superior to discussion for promoting factual learning but discussions to be superior to lectures for promoting higher-level reasoning, positive attitudes, and motivation to learn (McKeachie and Kulik 1975). Lecturing at best tends to focus on lower-level cognition. When the material is complex, detailed, or abstract, when students need to analyze, synthesize, or integrate the knowledge being studied, or when long-term retention is desired, lecturing is not a good idea. Formal cooperative learning groups should be used to accomplish such goals.

Fourth, lecturing is based on the assumption that all students need the same information, presented orally and impersonally, at the same pace, or without dialogue with the presenter. Even though students have different levels of knowledge about the subject being presented, lectures present the same information to all. The material covered in a lecture can often be communicated just as well in a text assignment or a handout. Lectures can waste students' time by telling them things they could read for themselves. While students learn and comprehend at different paces, a lecture proceeds at the lecturer's pace. While students who listen carefully and process the information cognitively will have questions that need to be answered, lectures typically are one-way streets of communication; further, the large number of classmates inhibits asking questions. And if students cannot ask questions, misconceptions, incorrect understanding, and gaps in understanding cannot be identified and corrected. A survey of over 1,000 college students, for example, found that, for 60 percent of the students, the presence of a large number of classmates would deter them from asking questions, even if the instructor encouraged them to do so (Stones 1970). Lecturing by its very nature impersonalizes learning.

Fifth, students tend not to like lecturing. A review of the literature indicates that students like the course and subject area better when they learn in discussion groups than when they learn by listening to lectures (Costin 1972)—an important factor in introductory courses where disciplines often attempt to attract majors.

Finally, lecturing is based on a series of assumptions about the cognitive capabilities and strategies of students. The lecturer assumes that all students learn auditorially, have high working memory capacity, have all the required prior knowledge, have good note-taking skills, and are not susceptible to information-processing overload.

Besides these problems with lecturing, certain obstacles make lectures less effective.

Student-centered barriers to lectures

A number of obstacles interfere with the effectiveness of a lecture:

1. *Preoccupation with what happened during the previous hour or on the way to class.* For lectures to succeed, faculty must take students' attention away from events in the hallway or on campus and focus their attention on the subject area and topic being dealt with in class.
2. *Emotional moods that block learning and cognitive processing of information.* Students who are angry or frustrated about something are not open to new learning. For lectures to work, faculty must set a mood conducive to learning.
3. *Students' disinterest, manifested by their going to sleep, turning on a tape recorder, writing letters, or reading a newspaper.* For lectures to work, faculty must focus students' attention on the material being presented and ensure that they cognitively process the information, integrating it into what they already know.
4. *Failure to understand the material being presented.* Students can learn material incorrectly and incompletely because they do not understand it. To make lectures work, some means must be available to check the accuracy and completeness of students' understanding of the material presented.

5. *Feelings of isolation and alienation and beliefs that no one cares about them as individuals, or about their academic progress.* To make lectures work, students have to believe that other people in the class will help because they care about the students as people and about the quality of their learning.
6. *Entertaining and clear lectures that students think they understand but actually misrepresent the complexity of the material.* While entertaining and impressing students are nice, they often do not help students understand and think critically about complex material. To make lectures work, students must think critically and use higher-level reasoning to cognitively process course content.

After considering these problems and barriers, one might conclude that alternative teaching strategies must be interwoven with lectures if lectures are to be effective. While lecturing and direct teaching have traditionally been conducted within competitive and individualistic structures, lectures can be made cooperative. Perhaps the major procedure to interweave with lecturing is the informal cooperative learning group.

Informal Cooperative Learning Groups
For lecturing to be successful and to overcome the obstacles to effective lecturing, students must become active cognitively. In what traditionally has been a passive learning environment for students, instructors must activate the learner through cooperative interaction with peers.

Informal cooperative learning groups are temporary, ad hoc groups that last for only one discussion or one class period. Their purposes are to focus students' attention on the material to be learned, to set a mood conducive to learning, to help organize in advance the material to be covered in class, to ensure that students cognitively process the material being taught, and to provide closure to an instructional session. Informal cooperative learning groups also ensure that misconceptions, incorrect understanding, and gaps in understanding are identified and corrected and that learning experiences are personalized. They can be used at any time, but they are especially useful during a lecture or direct teaching.

During lecturing and direct teaching, the instructional challenge for the teacher is to ensure that students do the intellectual work of organizing material, explaining it, summarizing it, and integrating it into existing conceptual networks. This goal can be achieved by having students do the advance organizing, cognitively process what they are learning, and provide closure to the lesson. Breaking up lectures with short cooperative processing times gives the instructor slightly less lecture time but helps counter what is proclaimed as the main problem of lectures: The information passes from the notes of the professor to the notes of the student without passing through the mind of either one.

Lecturing with Informal Cooperative Learning Groups

The following procedure helps to plan a lecture that keeps students more actively engaged intellectually. It entails using *focused discussions* before and after the lecture ("bookends") and interspersing *pair discussions* throughout the lecture. Two important aspects of using informal cooperative learning groups are to make the task and the instructions explicit and precise and to require the groups to produce a specific product (such as a written answer).

Listening to students' discussions can give the instructor direction and insight into how well students are grasping the concepts being taught.

1. *Introductory focused discussion.* Assign students to pairs. The nearest person will do, but the instructor might want to require different seating arrangements each class period so that students meet and interact with a number of other students in the class. Give the pairs four or five minutes to complete the initial (advance organizer) task. The discussion task is aimed at promoting advance organizing of what the students know about the topic to be presented and establishing expectations about what the lecture will cover.
2. *Lecture segment 1.* Deliver the first segment of the lecture, which should last from 10 to 15 minutes, about the length of time an adult can concentrate on a lecture.
3. *Pair discussion 1.* Give the students a discussion task focused on the material just presented that can be completed within three or four minutes. Its purpose is to ensure that students are actively thinking about the material being presented. The discussion task might be to answer a question posed by the instructor, react to the theory, concepts, or information being presented, or elaborate on the material being presented by relating it to past

learning so that it is integrated into existing conceptual frameworks. Discussion pairs respond to the task by (1) having each student formulate his or her answer; (2) sharing their answers with their partners; (3) listening carefully to the partner's answer; and (4) together creating a new answer that is superior to each member's initial formulation through the process of association, building on each other's thoughts, and synthesizing. The instructor then *randomly* chooses two or three students to give 30-second summaries of their discussions. Random selection ensures that the pairs take the tasks seriously and check each other so that both are prepared to answer.

4. *Lecture segment 2.* Deliver the second segment of the lecture.

5. *Pair discussion 2.* Give a discussion task focused on the second part of the lecture.

6. *Repetition.* Repeat this sequence of lecture and pair discussion until the lecture is completed.

7. *Closure-focused discussion.* Give an ending discussion task to summarize what students have learned from the lecture. Students should have four or five minutes to summarize and discuss the material covered in the lecture. The discussion should result in students' integrating what they have just learned into existing conceptual frameworks. The task could also point students toward what the homework will cover or what will be presented in the next class session. Doing so provides closure to the lecture.

The procedure should be used regularly to help students increase their skill and speed in completing short discussion tasks. Processing questions might cover how well prepared students were to complete the discussion tasks and how they could come better prepared to the next class session.

Informal cooperative learning groups also provide time for instructors to gather their wits, reorganize their notes, take a deep breath, and move around the class listening to what students are saying. Listening to students' discussions can give the instructor direction and insight into how well students are grasping the concepts being taught.

The following subsections present more specific procedures for the initial focused discussion, intermittent pair discussions, and the closure-focused discussion.

Introductory Focused Discussion

At the beginning of a class session, students could be required to meet in a permanent base group or in ad hoc informal cooperative discussion pairs or triads to review their homework and establish expectations about what the class session will focus on. Three ways of structuring such informal cooperative learning groups are discussion pairs, peer critiques of papers prepared in advance, and question-and-answer pairs.

Introductory focused discussion pairs

To prepare for the class session, students might be required to complete a short initial focused discussion task. The lecture could be planned around a series of questions answered in the lecture. The questions should be prepared on an overhead transparency or written on the board so that students can see them. Working cooperatively, students discuss the questions in pairs. The discussion task is aimed at promoting advance organization of what the students know about the topic to be presented and what the lecture will cover.

Introductory preparation paper

To prepare for each class session, students could be required to complete a short writing assignment. Even if it is not graded, it compels them to organize their thoughts and take some responsibility for the class's progress. Before each class session, students choose a major theory, concept, research study, or theorist/researcher discussed in the assigned reading and write a two-page analysis, summarizing the relevant assigned reading and adding material from another source to enrich their analysis. They then bring two copies of the paper to class. The members of their base group or discussion pair read, edit, and criticize the paper, using the following criteria. Does each paper have:

1. An introductory paragraph that outlines the content of the paper?
2. A clear conceptual definition of concepts and terms?
3. A summary of and judgment about what is known empirically (R = Substantial Research Support, r = some research support)?
4. A description of and judgment about theoretical significance (T = Substantial Theoretical Significance, t = some theoretical significance)?

5. A description of and judgment about practical significance (P = Substantial Practical Significance, p = some practical significance)?
6. A brief description of relevant research study that should be conducted?
7. New information beyond what is contained in the assigned readings?

Question-and-answer pairs

Question-and-answer pairs alternate asking and answering questions on the assigned reading:

1. To prepare for the discussion, students read an assignment and write questions dealing with the major points raised in the assigned reading or other related materials.
2. At the beginning of each class, students are randomly assigned to pairs, and one person (Student A) is chosen randomly to ask the first question.
3. The partner (Student B) answers. Student A can correct B's answer or give additional information.
4. Student B then asks the first member a question, and the process is repeated.
5. During this time, the instructor goes from pair to pair, giving feedback and asking and answering questions.

A variation of this procedure is the *jigsaw,* in which each student reads or prepares different materials. Each member of the group then teaches the material to the other member or members and vice versa (see also Goldschmid 1971).

Progress checks

Students can be given a progress check (similar to a quiz but not graded) consisting of questions (multiple choice, short answer, essay) that test students' knowledge of the assigned reading. Students individually complete the progress check, retake the progress check and compare answers with a partner from their base group, and, if time permits, retake the progress check in the whole base group to broaden the discussion of each question. For any question that they do not agree on, students should identify the page number and paragraph in the text where the correct answer can be found.

Intermittent Pair Discussions

Discussions among all the members of a class rarely involve many students. An observational study of instructor-student interaction found that when instructors attempted to solicit students' participation through questioning the whole class, students responded only 50 percent of the time (Barnes 1980). And when faculty manage to obtain students' participation, a very small minority of the students tends to dominate. In classes of fewer than 40 students, for example, four or five students accounted for 75 percent of all interaction, and, in classes with more than 40 students, two or three students accounted for over half of the exchanges (Karp and Yoels 1987).

Students often say, "I understood it at the time, but I do not remember it now." Experimental research on human memory (Keppel and Underwood 1962; Waugh and Norman 1965) indicates that two types of interference, retroactive and proactive, build up to cause forgetting during long periods of uninterrupted information processing, such as an hour-long lecture. *Retroactive* interference occurs when the information processed toward the end of the lecture interferes with the retention of the information processed at the beginning of the lecture; *proactive* interference occurs when the information processed at the beginning of the lecture interferes with retention of information processed at the end. The rehearsal of information soon after it has been received or processed results in greater retention of that information (Atkinson and Shiffrin 1971; Broadbent 1970), because the rate of human forgetting is sharpest immediately after the information is received. If the information is rehearsed orally soon after its reception, however, the brain has an opportunity to consolidate or lock in the memory trace, offsetting the rapid rate of forgetting. Interspersing pair discussions throughout the lecture avoids such long periods of uninterrupted listening and information processing, thus minimizing retroactive and proactive interference and enhancing students' retention of information presented in the lecture. In addition, pair discussions provide the opportunity for students to receive from classmates frequent and immediate feedback regarding their performance, increasing students' motivation to learn (Mackworth 1970).

Evidence suggests that college students do their best in courses that include frequent checkpoints of what they know, especially when the checkpoints occur in small cooperative groups. A study was conducted on the use of cooperative discussion pairs in combination with lecturing in separate courses over two semesters (Ruhl, Hughes, and Schloss 1987). In the two experimental classes, the instructor paused for two minutes three times during each of five lectures, with the intervals of lecturing between the two-minute pauses ranging from 12 to 18 minutes. During the pauses, no interaction occurred between instructor and students. The students worked in pairs to discuss and rework the notes they took during the lecture. The instructor gave two types of tests: immediate free-recall tests at the end of each lecture (students were given three minutes to write down everything they could remember from the lecture) and a 65-item multiple-choice test measuring long-term retention (administered 12 days after the final lecture). A control group received the same lectures without the pauses and were tested in the same manner. In both courses, students who engaged in the pair discussions achieved significantly higher on both tests than students who did not. The eight-point difference in the means between the experimental and control groups was large enough to make a difference of up to two letter grades, depending on the cut-off points.

During the lecture, the instructor stops every 10 to 15 minutes and gives students a short discussion task that students can complete in three or four minutes. Such a use of informal cooperative learning groups ensures that students are actively thinking about the material being presented. This procedure can be accomplished through several types of pairing.

Simultaneous explanation pairs
When a teacher asks a class for the answer and one student is chosen to respond, that student has an opportunity to clarify and extend what he or she knows through explaining, but only that student is involved and active. The rest of the class is passive. A teacher can ensure that all students are active by using a procedure that requires all students to explain their answers simultaneously. When each student has to explain his or her answer and reasoning to a classmate, all students are active and involved; no one is allowed to be passive. Simultaneous explaining can be structured in two basic ways: (1) Individual students formulate an answer and then explain it to a classmate, or (2) a small group formulates an answer and each member explains the group's answer and reasoning to a member of another group.

The task is for each student to explain his or her answers and reasoning to a classmate. The cooperative goal is to create a joint answer within a pair. Knowledge must be communicated to another person as soon as possible after it is learned.

Cooperative note-taking pairs

The notes a student takes during a lecture are of great importance in understanding what that student learns. In fact, most of the research on lecturing has focused on the value of taking notes, distinguishing between the encoding function (that is, taking notes assists learning from lectures) and the storage function (that is, reviewing notes is helpful) (Anderson and Armbruster 1982). Taking notes during lectures has been shown to be more effective than listening, but using the notes for review is more important than the mere fact of taking notes (Kiewra 1985b).

Students often take incomplete notes (Hartley and Marshall 1974; Kiewra 1985a) for several reasons:

1. Students with low working memory capacity have difficulty taking notes during lectures, possibly because they find it difficult to remember the information available in memory while writing it down (Kiewra and Benton 1988).
2. A student's information-processing load during a lecture is increased when the student has little prior knowledge of the information (White and Tisher 1986). When the lecturer uses visual aids frequently, a student can become overloaded from the pressure to take notes from visual presentations in addition to verbal statements.
3. Students who are unskilled in taking notes might take incomplete notes.
4. Students could have a false sense of familiarity with the material presented and therefore not bother taking notes.

To improve learning from lectures, students might focus on increasing the quantity and quality of the notes they take and/or improving their methods of reviewing the notes they have taken. Research on improving the quantity and quality of notes taken during lectures has often focused on the stimulating characteristics of the lecture itself (for example, the pace of the lecture, the use of advance organizers) or on the characteristics of the lecturer (White and Tisher 1986).

Cooperative note-taking pairs are a tool for structuring students' active cognitive processing during lectures and reducing their information-processing load. Two students work together with the common goal of mastering the information being presented. After exposure to a segment of the lecture, one partner summarizes his or her notes to the other, who in turn adds and corrects information. Students might ask each other, "What do you have in your notes so far?" "What are the three key points the instructor made?" "What was the most surprising thing the instructor said?" Such a procedure results in students' immediately rehearsing and more deeply processing the information, leading to better retention, and students' making multiple passes through the material, cognitively processing the information they are learning, and explicitly using metacognitive strategies. When students are provided with the instructor's lecture notes for review, performance is improved.

Read-and-explain pairs

Reading material given to students can be read in cooperative pairs more effectively than by individuals. Students should be assigned to pairs and given the task of establishing the meaning of each paragraph and then integrating the meaning of the paragraphs into the meaning of the whole. The cooperative goal (positive interdependence) is for both members to become experts on the assigned material. Students are to agree on the meaning of each paragraph, formulate one summary, and be able to explain the meaning of their answer according to the following procedure:

1. Both students silently read the first paragraph, and student A summarizes the content to student B.
2. They identify the question being asked in the paragraph.
3. They agree on a summary of the paragraph that answers the question.
4. They relate the meaning of the paragraph to previous learning.
5. They move to the next paragraph and repeat the procedure.

Teaching concepts inductively

Concepts can be taught inductively as well as deductively. Concepts can be formed inductively by instructing students to figure out why the examples have been placed in different boxes. One procedure for doing so is as follows:

1. Draw two (or three) boxes on the chalkboard and label them "Box 1" and "Box 2."
2. Place one item in each box.
3. Instruct pairs of students to formulate, explain, listen, and create to discuss how the items are different.
4. Place another item in each box and repeat the procedure, telling the pairs of students not to say out loud to another group or the class how the items are different. Each pair must discover it.
5. Once a pair has the answer, the members are to make a definition for each box. They then create new examples that can be placed in the boxes.

Requesting active responses
A number of other strategies using active responses can be used as part of a lecture. They include asking students to indicate their answer or opinion by raising their hands, putting thumbs up or thumbs down, or clapping once if they agree.

Closure-Focused Discussion
After the lecture has ended, students should work in small discussion groups to reconstruct the lecture conceptually. A number of research studies conducted in the 1920s document students' forgetting curve for material presented in the lecture (Menges 1988). The average student demonstrated immediate recall of 62 percent of the material presented in the lecture, but that recall declined to 45 percent after three to four days and fell to 24 percent after eight weeks. If students were asked to take an examination immediately after the lecture (systematically reviewing what they had just learned), however, they retained almost twice as much information, both factual and conceptual, after eight weeks. Other types of systematic reviews, such as focused discussions and writing assignments, should have similar effects on the retention of the material presented.

Closure for focused discussion
At the end of the lecture, students should discuss the content of the lecture. They should have four or five minutes to summarize and discuss the material covered in the lecture. The

discussion should result in students' integrating what they have just learned into existing conceptual frameworks. The task might also point students toward what the homework will cover or what will be presented in the next class. Doing so provides closure to the lecture. For example, the pairs of students could be asked to list the five most important things they learned and two questions they would like to ask. The instructor collects the answers and records them to support the importance of the procedure and to see what students have learned. Handing the papers back periodically with brief comments from the instructor helps reinforce this procedure for students.

Closure for cooperative writing pairs
Faculty benefit from asking students to write a one-minute paper at the end of each teaching session describing the major point they learned and the main unanswered question they still have (Light 1990). Doing so helps students to focus on the central themes of the course. In writing their papers, students should first write an introductory paragraph that outlines the content of the lecture, clear conceptual definitions of concepts and terms presented, a summary of and judgment about the information presented, a description of and judgment about theoretical significance of the information presented, a description of and judgment about practical significance, and anything the student knows beyond what was covered in the lecture.

Closure for note-taking pairs
Closure for note-taking pairs is similar to the cooperative note-taking pairs used intermittently during the lecture. Students review and complete their lecture notes, reflecting on the lecture, and write the major concepts and pertinent information presented. More specifically, two students work together with the common goal of mastering the information being presented. After the lecture, one partner summarizes his or her notes to the other, who in turn adds and corrects. Students can ask each other what they have in their notes, the three key points the instructor made, and the most surprising thing the instructor said.

Implementation assignment
Students might be asked to make a specific contract with their base group about how they will apply what they have learned.

At the end of the class session, each member plans how to apply what he or she learned. Each member discusses with the group and then writes down three specific answers to two questions: What have I learned? and How will I use it? In planning how to implement what they have learned, it is important that the instructor be as specific as possible about plans for implementation and keep a careful record of efforts to implement the information.

Other Informal Cooperative Learning Groups

Bookends for films or demonstrations
A demonstration is the modeling of skills or procedures. Informal cooperative learning groups can be used whenever the instructor gives a demonstration, shows a film, or has a guest speaker. Informal cooperative learning groups are very useful in setting an anticipatory set for the demonstration before it begins and processing what was learned from the demonstration afterward.

Peer feedback groups
Students like courses that offer frequent opportunities to revise and improve their work as they go along. They learn best when they have a chance to submit an early version of their work, get detailed feedback and criticism, and then hand in a final version for a grade. While this procedure can most easily be followed for writing assignments, it also works for quizzes, tests, brief papers, and oral examinations.

Cooperative study groups
The Harvard assessment seminars compared the grades of students who studied alone with those of students who studied in groups of four to six (Light 1990). Invariably, the students who studied in small groups did better than those who studied alone. The students in small study groups spoke more often, asked more questions, and were generally more engaged than those in the larger groups.

Conclusions
The sage on the stage talks without interruption. The guide has students talk. When direct teaching procedures, such as lecturing, are used, informal cooperative learning groups can be used to focus students' attention on the material to be learned, set a mood conducive to learning, help set expec-

Informal cooperative learning groups can be used whenever the instructor gives a demonstration, shows a film, or has a guest speaker.

tations about what will be covered in a class session, ensure that students cognitively process the material being taught, keep students' attention focused on the content, ensure that misconceptions, incorrect understanding, and gaps in understanding are corrected, provide an opportunity for discussion and elaboration that promote retention and transfer, make learning experiences personal and immediate, and provide closure to an instructional session. Students can summarize in three to five minutes what they know about a topic before and after a lecture. Five-minute discussions in cooperative pairs can be interspersed throughout a lecture. Thus, the main problem of lectures, that information passes from the notes of the professor to the notes of the student without passing through the mind of either one, can be countered.

The following section discusses the need for a permanent base group that provides relatively long-term relationships among students.

BASE GROUPS

*The biggest disease today is not leprosy or tuberculosis, but
rather the feeling of being unwanted, uncared for, and
deserted by everybody.*
　　　　　—Mother Teresa, Nobel Peace Prize winner, 1979

Any student who enters college needs two types of support
groups: an *academic support group* that provides any needed
assistance and helps students succeed academically in college
and a *personal support group* made up of people who care
about and are personally committed to the student. At most
colleges, students are expected to develop these support systems on their own. College and university life, however, can
be lonely. Many students arrive on campus without a clear
support group. They can attend class without ever talking to
other students. In such impersonal settings, base groups are
important.

For many reasons, colleges might wish to use cooperative
base groups to structure students into both types of support
systems. It is important that some of the relationships built
within cooperative learning groups be permanent. College
has to be more than a series of temporary encounters that
last for only a semester. College students should be assigned
to permanent base groups to create permanent committed
relationships with classmates who will provide the support,
help, encouragement, and assistance students need to make
academic progress and develop cognitively and socially. This
section first defines base groups and then details how they
can be used to provide a permanent support system for each
student.

What Are Base Groups?

Base groups:

1. Have heterogeneous membership so that they represent
   a cross section of the school's population in terms of
   gender, ability, and ethnic and cultural background.
2. Last for the duration of the class (a semester or year) and
   preferably from the freshman through the senior year.
   When students know that the cooperative base group will
   stay together until each member is graduated, they
   become committed to finding ways to motivate and
   encourage the other members of the group. Problems in
   working with each other cannot be ignored or waited out.

3. Meet regularly.
4. Personalize the work required and the learning experiences.

Base groups' purposes are for members to provide each other with the support, encouragement, and assistance needed to complete assignments and to progress academically, including letting absent members know what went on in class and interacting informally every day during and between classes, discussing assignments, and helping each other with homework; and to hold each other accountable for striving to make academic progress.

Effective base groups use several key ingredients. First, formal cooperative learning groups for instructional purposes should be used frequently until the five essential elements discussed earlier are understood and students have gained some expertise in using cooperative learning groups. Second, base groups should be slightly larger than formal cooperative learning groups (base groups can have four or five members rather than two or three). Third, students should not be assigned to base groups the first day of class but after a few days when the instructor begins to know the students somewhat and the class's membership stabilizes. Fourth, meetings of base groups should be scheduled frequently. Fifth, an important agenda should be planned for each meeting. The agenda can include:

1. *Academic support tasks,* such as checking to see what assignments each member has and what help he or she needs to complete them. Members can give each other advice on how to take tests and "survive" in school, prepare each other to take tests and go over the questions missed afterward, and share their areas of expertise with each other. Above all, members monitor each other's academic progress and make sure all members are achieving.
2. *Routine tasks,* such as taking roll or collecting homework.
3. *Personal support tasks,* such as listening sympathetically when a member has problems with parents or friends, discussing life in general, giving each other advice about relationships, and helping each other solve nonacademic problems. Teachers can increase the likelihood of personal support by conducting trust-building exercises with the base groups, such as members' sharing their favorite

movie, a childhood experience, or a memory from high school.

Finally, some base groups can be expected to have problematic relationships. Not all base groups cohere right away. The instructor should be ready to help unskilled members integrate themselves into their groups by periodically structuring a meeting of the base group to process the relationships among members or give the group hypothetical problems to solve ("What if one member of your group talked 90 percent of the time? What are three strategies to help him or her listen as well as contribute?"). Persistence and patience are good qualities for instructors with poorly functioning base groups.

Procedures
Base groups can be used at the college level in two ways. The first is to have a base group in each college course that stays together only for the duration of the course. The second is to organize all students within the college into base groups and have the groups function as an essential component of college life. College base groups stay together for at least a year, preferably for four years or until all members are graduated.

Class base groups
The larger or more impersonal the class and the more complex the subject matter, the more important it is to use base groups. The members of base groups should exchange phone numbers and information about schedules, as they might want to meet outside of class. The class base group functions as a support group for members:

1. Giving assistance, support, and encouragement for mastering the course content and skills, and providing feedback on how well the content and skills are being learned;
2. Giving assistance, support, and encouragement for thinking critically about the course content, explaining precisely what one learns, engaging in intellectual controversy, getting the work done on time, and applying what is learned to one's own life;
3. Providing a set of interpersonal relationships to personalize the course and an arena for trying out the cooper-

ative learning procedures and skills emphasized in the course; and

4. Providing a structure for managing course procedures, such as homework, attendance, and evaluation.

Members of class base groups are responsible for mastering and implementing the theories, concepts, and skills emphasized in the course, and for ensuring that all members of the base group and the class do likewise. If the group is successful, members should find another group to help until all members of the class are successful. Cooperation, not competition, among groups is key.

At the beginning of each session, class members meet in their base groups to:

1. Congratulate each other for living through the time since the last class session and check to see that no one is under undue stress. The two questions to discuss are "How are you today?" and "Are we all prepared for this class period?"

2. Check to see whether members have completed their homework or need help to do so. The questions to discuss are "Did you do your homework?" and "Is there anything you did not understand?" If no time is available to help each other during the base group meeting, an appointment is made to meet again during free time or lunch. Periodically, the base groups can be given a checklist of academic skills and assess which ones each member needs to practice more.

3. Review what members have read and done since the last class session. Members should be able to briefly and succinctly summarize what they have read, thought about, and done. They could come to class with resources they have found and want to share or copies of work they have completed and want to distribute to the members of their group.

4. Get to know each other better and provide positive feedback by discussing such questions as, "What do you like about each other and yourself?" and "What is the best thing that happened to you this week?"

Class base groups are available to support individual group members. If a group member arrives late or must leave early on occasion, the group can provide information about what that student missed. Additionally, group members can assist each other in writing required papers. Base groups can discuss assignments, plan, review, and edit papers, and address any questions regarding course assignments and class sessions. If the group is not able to resolve the issue, then it should be brought to the instructor's or teaching assistant's attention.

All members are expected to contribute actively to the class discussion, work to maintain effective working relationships with other participants, complete all assignments, assist class-mates in completing their assignments, express their ideas, not change their minds unless they are persuaded by logic or information to do so, and indicate agreement with the base group's work by signing the weekly contract.

The importance of class base groups cannot be overemphasized. In the early 1970s, for example, a graduate student taking a course in the social psychology of education suffered a psychological breakdown and was hospitalized for most of the quarter in a locked psychiatric ward of a local hospital. Two years later, she thanked the instructor for the course, stating that it was the only course she had completed that very difficult year. The other members of her base group had obtained permission from her psychiatrist to visit her weekly in the hospital. They spent two hours a week with her, going over her assignments, helping her write her papers, giving her the tests, and ensuring that she completed the course. She got a "B."

College base groups

At the beginning of the academic year, students should be assigned to base groups. Class schedules should be arranged so that members of base groups are assigned to as many of the same classes as possible. Members will then spend much of the day together. In essence, the computer is programmed to assign base groups to classes (whenever possible) rather than to individuals. Base groups should stay together for at least a year, ideally for four.

Some attention should be paid to building identity and cohesion for the group. The first week the base groups meet, for example, base groups can pick a name, design a flag, or choose a motto. If an instructor in the school has the proper expertise, the groups will benefit from participating in a "challenge course" involving ropes and obstacles. This type of physical challenge builds cohesion quickly.

During the year, base groups meet either twice each day or twice each week or some variation in between. When base groups meet twice each day, they meet first thing in the morning and last thing in the afternoon. At the beginning of each day, students meet in their base groups to:

1. Congratulate each other for showing up with all their books and materials and check to see that none of their members are under undue stress. The two questions to discuss are "How are you today?" and "Are we all prepared for the day?"
2. Check to see whether members are keeping up with their work in their classes or need help in doing so. The topics for discussion are "How are you doing in each of your classes?" and "Is there anything you did not understand?" If not enough time is available to help each other during the base group's meeting, members make an appointment to meet again during free time or lunch. Periodically, the base groups can be given a checklist of academic skills and assess which ones each member needs to practice more.
3. Review what members have read and done since the day before. Members should be able to briefly and succinctly summarize what they have read, thought about, and done. They might come to class with resources they have found and want to share or copies of work they have completed and want to distribute to the members of their group.
4. Get to know each other better and provide positive feedback by discussing such questions as "What do you like about each other and yourself?" and "What is the best thing that happened to you this past week?"

At the end of the day, members meet in their base groups to see that all members are taking their homework home, understand the assignments to be completed, and have the help they need to do their work (during the evening, students can confer on the telephone or study together at one house). In addition, base groups might want to discuss what members have learned during the day and check to see whether all members have plans to do something fun and interesting that evening.

When base groups meet twice each week (perhaps first thing on Monday and last thing on Friday), they meet to discuss the academic progress of each member, provide assistance for each other, and hold each member accountable for completing assignments and progressing satisfactorily through the academic program. The meeting on Monday morning refocuses the students on school, provides any emotional support required after the weekend, reestablishes personal contact among base group members, and helps students set their academic goals for the week (what is still to be done on assignments and so forth). Members should carefully review each other's assignments and ensure that members have the help needed. In addition, they should hold each other accountable for making a serious effort to succeed in school. The meeting on Friday afternoon helps students review the week, set academic goals for the weekend, and share plans and hopes for the weekend.

Why Use Cooperative Base Groups?

Hold onto what is good
  Even if it is a handful of earth
Hold onto what you believe in
  Even if it is a tree which stands by itself
Hold onto what you must do
  Even if it is a long way from here
Hold onto life
  Even if it is easier to let go
Hold onto my hand
  Even when I have gone away from you
—Pueblo Indian Poem

Cooperative base groups should be used in college for many reasons. One major outcome of cooperative learning is that students who work together to get the job done develop positive relationships with each other. The longer the group is together, the more positive and personal the relationships among members. The caring and committed relationships built in base groups are essential for motivating long-term efforts to achieve and for healthy social, cognitive, and physical development. The development of academically oriented values depends on long-term caring relationships.

The need for long-term permanent relationships

Most relationships in college are, at best, shipboard romances. When most instructors face their classes and when most classmates look at each other, they implicitly say, "I will know you for the duration of this course." Students know that next semester or year they will have a different instructor and different classmates. Relationships are temporary because in most colleges it is assumed that any classmate and any instructor will do. Classmates and instructors are perceived to be replaceable parts in the education machine. It is assumed that a student's instructors and classmates are basically irrelevant to the educational process.

It is important, however, that some of the relationships built in college be permanent. Receiving social support and being held accountable for appropriate behavior by peers who care and have a long-term commitment to one's success and well-being are important aspects of progressing through college. They increase achievement and promote psychological health. Permanent relationships mean increased opportunity to transmit achievement-oriented values. Learning for one's caring and committed groupmates is a powerful motivator. Thus, permanent cooperative base groups can be formed to create the caring and committed relationships that improve attendance, personalize the experience at school, increase achievement, and improve the quality of life in the classroom.

Accountability and motivation

Education is not successful unless each student is working hard to do his or her best. Not everyone has a high IQ or complex talents, but every student can work hard to maximize his or her achievements, conceptual understanding of the material being studied, level of reasoning, and creativity. Numerous students, however, spend very little time studying, even those students who get good grades. Students often avoid hard subjects like math, science, and foreign languages and simply coast, doing far less than they are capable of doing.

To increase the effort students commit to learning and achievement, they must be involved in caring and committed relationships within which they are held accountable for exerting considerable effort to learn and given the help, encouragement, and recognition they need to sustain their efforts to achieve. Long-term, hard, persistent efforts to achieve come from the heart, not from the head. When faced with the choice to watch television or do their homework, the decision might be based more on emotional than intellectual grounds. No motivator is more powerful than students' realizing that they have to turn off the television and do their schoolwork because the group is counting on them. Many students who could care less what an instructor thinks will say, "I did my homework because I couldn't face my group and tell them I didn't do it. I couldn't let my group down."

Changing students' attitudes about academic work
Many students do not value schoolwork, do not aspire to do well in college, do not plan to take difficult courses, and plan to just get by. One of the responsibilities of faculty is to change such attitudes so that students value school, education, and hard work to learn. Several general principles, supported by research, guide the faculty member's efforts:

1. Attitudes are changed in groups, not individually. Focus efforts on having students in small groups persuade each other to value education.
2. Attitudes are changed as a result of small-group discussions that lead to public commitment to work harder in school and take education more seriously. Attitudes are rarely modified by information or preaching.
3. Messages from individuals who care about, and are committed to, the student are taken more seriously than messages from indifferent others. Committed and caring relationships should be built between academically oriented and nonacademically oriented students.
4. Appeals to value education should be personally tailored to the individual student. General messages are not nearly as effective as personal messages. The individuals best able to construct an effective personal appeal are peers who know the student well.
5. Conversions are long term, not sudden. Internalizing academic values will take years of persuasion by caring and committed peers.
6. Support from caring and committed peers is essential to modifying attitudes and behaviors and maintaining the new ones. Students cannot do it alone; they need help from their friends (see Johnson and F. Johnson 1991).

Students might best be encouraged to value education, work hard in school, take the valuable but difficult courses,

Long-term, hard, persistent efforts to achieve come from the heart, not from the head.

and aspire to go to graduate school by being placed in permanent base groups that provide members with help and encouragement and hold members accountable for working hard in college. The base group provides a setting to encourage academic values and the necessary caring and committed relationships.

Base groups and dropping out of college

In many colleges, large numbers of students drop out, especially during the freshman year. Base groups provide a means of preventing and combating dropping out. Students who believe that no one knows or cares about them or would miss them when they leave are at risk of dropping out. Base groups provide a set of personal and supportive relationships that could prevent many students from dropping out of college. Dropping out often results from being alienated from the college and other students. Base groups also provide a means of fighting a student's inclination to drop out. A faculty member might approach a base group and say, "Roger thinks he is dropping out of college. Go find and talk to him. We're not going to lose him without a fight."

The necessities of life

All students need to develop certain basics in life in healthy ways. One set of necessities involves good nutrition, adequate sleep, and appropriate clothing and shelter. Another set involves caring and committed relationships. All students need to know that certain people are committed to them and will help them when needed. Colleges need to ensure that every student is involved in such relationships with peers. One way to do so is through cooperative base groups.

The Adviser/Advisee Base Group

In many colleges, it will seem difficult to implement base groups. One opportunity is adviser/advisee groups. Instructors might divide their advisees into base groups and then plan an important agenda for them to follow during a daily or a weekly meeting. They could then meet once a week for 30 minutes with all of the advisees, with the base groups given four tasks:

1. A quick self-disclosure task, such as "What is the most exciting thing you plan during winter break?" "What is

the worst thing that happened to you last weekend?"
"What is your biggest fear?" "What is your favorite ice
cream?"
2. An administrative task, such as registration for next
semester.
3. An academic task, such as writing three pieces of advice
for taking midterms as a group. Then suggestions from
each group can be handed out the following week.
4. A closing task, such as wishing each other good luck for
the day or the week.

Conclusion

The coordinated use of cooperative formal, informal, and base
groups provides the basis for educating college students. As
students spend more and more time in cooperative learning
groups, however, the competitive/individualistic relationships
among faculty become more apparent and less defensible.
What is good for students is even better for faculty. The next
section discusses cooperation among faculty.

COOPERATION AMONG FACULTY

The Organizational Structure of Colleges

To have joy one must share it. Happiness was born a twin.
—Indian proverb

What is good for students is even better for faculty. The research that validates the use of cooperative learning in the classroom also validates the use of cooperative faculty teams at the departmental or college level. The use of cooperative learning, furthermore, is promoted when the organizational structure of the college is congruent with the instructional methods recommended.

Colleges are not buildings, curricula, and machines. They are relationships and interactions among people (Johnson and Johnson 1989c). How the interpersonal interaction is structured determines how effective colleges are. Faculty relationships can be structured in three ways: competitively, individualistically, and cooperatively. The faculty's effectiveness depends on interpersonal interactions that are oriented toward cooperative achievement of the college's goals. Colleges must be cooperative places. A cooperatively structured college consists of cooperative learning within the classroom and cooperative efforts within the faculty. In other words, the organizational structure of colleges must change from a competitive/individualistic mass-manufacturing structure within which faculty work alone to a high-performance, team-based organizational structure in which faculty work in teams. Such a change will not be easy in many cases, for the organizational structure of colleges traditionally has discouraged collegiality among instructors and severely limited their opportunities to cooperate with each other.

Colleges are loosely coupled organizations in which instructors and administrators function far more independently than interdependently, with little or no supervision, and engage in actions that do not determine or affect what others do and actions that seem isolated from their consequences (Johnson and Johnson 1989c). Instructors are systematically isolated from each other during most of the college day. And that isolation often results in instructors' experiencing an amorphous and diffuse competition with their peers.

To increase the cooperation among faculty, faculty members could be organized into three different types of cooperative teams: collegial support groups to encourage and support each other's efforts to use cooperative learning, task forces to recommend how to deal with collegewide issues, such as revising the curriculum, and ad hoc decision-making groups to involve all faculty members in important college decisions.

Collegial Support Groups

The success of a college largely depends on the success of instructors in educating students. And the success of instructors in educating students depends on how committed they are to continually increasing their instructional expertise and the amount of physical and psychological energy instructors commit to their work. The commitment of physical and psychological energy to achieve the goal of improving one's instructional expertise is heavily influenced by the degree to which colleagues are supportive and encouraging. Instructors generally teach better when they have support from their peers. In most colleges, however, such support is hard to achieve. As a result, instructors often feel harried, isolated, and alienated, although they need, as humans, to work cooperatively and intimately with supportive people. Collegial support groups provide instructors with the opportunity to share ideas, support each other's efforts to use cooperative learning, and encourage each other.

A collegial support group includes two to five instructors whose goal is to improve each other's instructional expertise and promote each other's professional growth (Johnson and Johnson 1989c). Collegial support groups should be small, and members should be heterogeneous. Collegial support groups are first and foremost safe places where members like to be; where support, caring, concern, laughter, camaraderie, and celebration are common; and where the primary goal of improving each other's competence in using cooperative learning is never obscured. The purpose of this collegial support group is to work jointly to improve continuously each other's expertise in using cooperative learning procedures or, in other words, to:

1. Provide the help, support, and encouragement each member needs to gain as high a level of expertise in using cooperative learning as possible;
2. Serve as an informal support group for sharing, letting off steam, and discussing problems connected with implementing cooperative learning;

3. Serve as a base for instructors experienced in the use of cooperative learning to teach other instructors how to structure and manage lessons cooperatively; and
4. Create a setting in which camaraderie and shared success are celebrated.

Collegial support groups succeed when they are carefully structured to ensure active participation by members and concrete products (such as lesson plans) that members can actually use. The structure must clearly point members toward increasing each other's expertise in implementing cooperative learning to prevent meetings from degenerating into gripe sessions, destructive criticism of each other, or amateur therapy. Members need to believe they sink or swim together, ensure considerable face-to-face discussion and assistance take place, hold each other accountable for implementing cooperative learning in between meetings, learn and use the interpersonal and small-group skills required to make meetings productive, and periodically initiate a discussion of how effective the collegial support group is in carrying out its mission. Task-oriented discussion, planning, and problem solving, and empathy and mutual support should dominate the meetings.

A collegial support group has three key activities:

1. Frequent professional discussions of cooperative learning in which information is shared, successes are celebrated, and problems connected with implementation are solved;
2. Coplanning, codesigning, copreparing, and coevaluating curricular materials relevant to implementing cooperative learning in the classrooms of the members;
3. Coteaching and reciprocal observations of each other teaching lessons structured cooperatively and jointly processing those observations (Little 1981).

Professional discussions
What most instructors find very useful is an opportunity to talk to each other about teaching. Within collegial support groups, frequent, continuous, increasingly concrete and precise talk takes place about the use of cooperative learning procedures. Through such discussion, members build a concrete, precise, and coherent shared language that can describe the complexity of using cooperative learning, distinguish one

practice and its virtues from another, and integrate cooperative learning into other teaching practices and strategies they are already using. Through such discussions, instructors can exchange successful strategies and materials, focusing on solving specific problems members might be having in perfecting their use of cooperative learning. Most of all, instructors' comprehension and deeper understanding of the nature of cooperative learning can be enhanced by explaining to their colleagues how they are implementing it.

Joint planning and curriculum design

Well begun is half done.

—Aristotle

Members of professional support groups should frequently plan, design, prepare, and evaluate lesson plans together. Doing so results in instructors' sharing the burden of developing materials needed to conduct cooperative lessons, generating emerging understanding of cooperative learning strategies, making realistic standards for students and colleagues, and providing the machinery for each other to implement cooperative learning. Instructors should leave each meeting of their collegial support group with something concrete that helps them to implement cooperative learning. The process of planning a lesson together, each conducting it, and then processing it afterward is often constructive. This cycle of coplanning, parallel teaching, and coprocessing can be followed by one of coplanning, coteaching, and coprocessing.

The discussions and coplanning that take place in collegial support groups ensure that instructors clarify their understanding of what cooperative learning is, and create a support and accountability system to ensure that they try it out. The next steps in increasing expertise are to assess the consequences of using cooperative learning, reflect on how well the lesson went, and teach another cooperative lesson in a modified way. All of these steps benefit from the input and feedback from supportive colleagues. The more colleagues are involved in one's teaching, the more valuable the help and assistance they can provide.

Reciprocal observations

Members of collegial support groups should frequently observe each other teaching lessons structured cooperatively and then provide each other with useful feedback. This process of observation and feedback provides members with shared experiences to discuss and refer to. Furthermore, the observation and feedback have to be reciprocal. Instructors especially need to treat each other with the deference that shows they recognize that anyone can have good and bad days and that the mistakes they note in a colleague could be the same mistakes they will make tomorrow.

Certain guidelines should be followed when observing the teaching of other members of the collegial support group:

1. Realize that it is possible to learn from every other member of the group, regardless of their experience and personal characteristics.
2. Make sure observation and feedback are reciprocal.
3. Ask the person being observed what he or she would like attention to be focused on. It might include specific students the teacher wants observed, specific aspects of structuring interdependence or accountability, or some other aspect of cooperative learning.
4. Focus feedback and comments on what has taken place, not on personal competence.
5. Do not confuse a teacher's personal worth with her or his current level of competence in using cooperative learning.
6. Be concrete and practical in discussions about how effectively members are using cooperative learning.
7. Above all, communicate respect for each other's overall competence in teaching. Recognize and respect professional strengths in others.

Working cooperatively with others brings with it camaraderie, friendship, warmth, satisfaction, and feelings of success. They are all to be enjoyed.

Collegewide Task Forces
For many collegewide issues (revising the curriculum, for example), task forces must be organized (Johnson and Johnson 1989c) to carefully consider and research the issue and make a recommendation to the faculty as a whole. To be effective, task forces must collect valid and complete information about the problem, engage in controversy to ensure that all alternative solutions are fairly heard, synthesize the best points

from all perspectives, and make a free and informed choice of which alternative to adopt. Members must have continuing motivation to solve the problem so that a new recommendation can be made if the initial plan does not work.

Ad Hoc Decision-Making Groups

At faculty meetings, ad hoc decision-making groups consider the recommendations of the task forces and decide whether to accept or modify the proposed solution (Johnson and Johnson 1989c). Faculty members are assigned to temporary cooperative decision-making groups of three during a faculty meeting. The ad hoc groups consider the recommendation of the task force and decide whether to accept or modify the recommendation. Each ad hoc group then reports its decision to the entire faculty, after which the faculty discusses it and then decides by consensus which solution is best.

Conclusion

Traditionally, instructors have not been skilled in working effectively with adult peers, lacking skills in teamwork and being too ready to resolve differences by voting or by following the leader (Blake and Mouton 1974). Educators are far less competent in working in small problem-solving groups than industrial personnel. Further, educators describe themselves as being more oriented toward compromising quality of work for harmonious relationships, exerting minimal effort to get the job done, and being more oriented toward keeping good relationships than toward achieving the college's goals. Instructors are ill-equipped behaviorally to function as part of a faculty, lacking the skills and attitudes needed for effective group problem solving (Blumberg, May, and Perry 1974).

The lack of competence in being a constructive colleague, however, is not primarily the fault of instructors. The competitive/individualistic organizational structure existing in most colleges discourages cooperation among faculty. To implement cooperative learning in college classrooms, it might also be necessary to implement cooperative teams among faculty. It is time that the college becomes a modern organization. In the real world, most of the important work is done by cooperative teams rather than by individuals. The structuring of cooperation among faculty would both support the use of cooperative learning and provide a congruent organizational structure throughout the college.

CONCLUSIONS

Whether one believes in a religion or not, and whether one believes in rebirth or not, there isn't anyone who doesn't appreciate kindness and compassion. . . . We must build closer relationships of mutual trust, understanding, respect, and help, irrespective of differences of culture, philosophy, religion, or faith.
    —The Dalai Lama, Nobel Peace Prize winner, 1989

"I want to be able to hear a pin drop in this room." "Don't copy." "I want to see what *you* can do, not your neighbor." "Save the talking for the hallway." These familiar statements exhort students to work by themselves without interacting with their classmates. In many classrooms, however, such statements are becoming passe. Throughout North America, Europe, the South Pacific, and many other parts of the world, colleges are rediscovering the power of having students work together to learn.

Considerable research demonstrates that cooperative learning produces higher achievement, more positive relationships among students, and healthier psychological adjustment than do competitive or individualistic experiences. These effects, however, do not automatically appear when students are placed in groups. To be cooperative, learning groups must be carefully structured to include the five basic elements: positive interdependence, face-to-face promotive interaction, individual accountability, social skills to work effectively with others, and group processing to reflect on and improve the quality of group work. And cooperative learning can be structured in many different ways. Three broad categories of cooperative learning strategies include *formal cooperative learning groups* that last for several class sessions to complete assignments, *informal cooperative learning groups* that last for only a few minutes for a brief discussion, and *cooperative base groups* that last for a semester or more to provide overall academic assistance. And cooperation is just as powerful among faculty as it is among students. The existing competitive/individualistic college structure must be reorganized to become a cooperative, team-based college structure.

Typical Cooperative Learning Class Sessions
In a typical class period, formal cooperative learning strategies, informal cooperative learning strategies, and cooperative base groups are all used in an integrated fashion to structure class sessions.

Fifty-minute class period

A typical class session consists of a meeting of the base group, a short lecture and/or a group project, and an ending meeting of the base group. The instructor formally starts the class by welcoming the students and instructing them to meet in their base groups. The introduction and warm-up for the class are provided in base groups. The initial meeting of the base group includes one or more of the following tasks for members: greeting each other, checking to see whether all members have completed their homework successfully or need help, and reviewing what members have read and done since the previous class session. The base group's activities must be completed within about five minutes. Regularly structuring this time is essential for helping students achieve a good mood for learning, communicating high expectations about completing homework and helping others, and providing a transition between the students' (and professor's) previous hour and the current class session.

In a 50-minute class session, the instructor usually has three choices: giving a lecture using informal cooperative learning groups, having students complete an assignment in formal cooperative learning groups, or presenting a short lecture and assigning a short group lesson. If a lecture is to be given, it begins and ends with a focused discussion in an informal cooperative learning group and has paired discussions interspersed throughout the lecture. During both types of discussions, students are asked to formulate, share, listen, and create:

1. *Formulate* an answer to the question or solution to the problem individually (one to two minutes);
2. *Share* that answer with the partner (one minute each);
3. *Listen* carefully to the partner's answer;
4. *Create* an answer through discussion that is superior to the individual answers (one to two minutes).

Students are slow and awkward when following this procedure initially, but once they become familiar with it, they work intensely. Again, it is an important time for the professor to circulate among students, listening and learning what they already know about the topic. In the long run, it is important to vary the type of informal cooperative learning groups, using simultaneous explanation pairs one day and cooperative note-taking pairs another.

If a group assignment is given, it is carefully structured to be cooperative. The instructor notes the objectives of the lesson, makes a series of preinstructional decisions, communicates the task and the positive interdependence, monitors the groups as they work and intervenes when needed, evaluates students' learning, and has groups process how effectively members are working together. Formal cooperative learning groups are used when the instructor wants to achieve an instructional objective that includes conceptual learning, problem solving, or the development of students' skills in critical thinking. Formal cooperative learning groups are needed for simulations of first-hand experiences, role playing, or the sharing of expertise and resources among members.

Summarizing and synthesizing must be structured in near the end of the class period. In a shorter class period, they might simply involve each student's working with his or her partner to create a list of three or four major lessons and one or two questions. Periodically, the professor can collect them. Quickly reading and commenting on these summaries provides the professor with valuable information about what the students are learning and what questions they have, and sends a message to the students that the activity is important.

Students are slow and awkward when following this procedure initially, but once they become familiar with it, they work intensely.

At the end of the class session, students meet in their base groups to summarize and synthesize what they have learned. Base groups can hand in a written summary of the new concept learned or elaborate by relating the new lesson to previously learned material or apply what they have learned to a practical situation. Finally, members of the base groups should celebrate their hard work and success. At the end of the class session, after working cooperatively, students (and the professor) often have the joyful feeling, "We did it." Students leave the class with an empowered sense, "Since we did it, I can do it."

Ninety-minute class session
The basic structure of a 90-minute period is basically the same as for the 50-minute period, except it is easier to both lecture and have cooperative learning groups complete an assignment in one class session. Class begins with a meeting of the base groups, after which the instructor lectures using informal cooperative learning groups to ensure that students are cognitively active while the instructor disseminates information, conducts a formal cooperative learning activity to promote problem solving and higher-level learning, and closes the

class with a second meeting of the base groups.

The meetings of the base groups can be longer (up to 15 minutes), involving more varied activities, such as reviewing papers prepared in advance or progress checks. Valuable information can be gleaned by eavesdropping on the base groups and noting which parts of the assignment cause difficulty.

A lecture might follow. When using a variety of procedures for informal cooperative learning groups, faculty need to structure carefully the five basic elements of cooperative learning in the learning situation.

Formal cooperative learning groups become the heart of longer class periods. Students take increasing responsibility for each other's learning, and the professor takes increasing responsibility for guiding this process. Faculty should structure positive interdependence in a variety of ways and give students the opportunity to promote each other's learning face to face. It is helpful to use a variety of formal cooperative learning procedures, such as jigsaw classes, problem solving, joint projects, and peer composition. Occasional reporting by the students to the whole class (by randomly calling on individual students to report for their group) can help the professor guide the overall flow of the class. Carefully monitoring the cooperative groups and using formal observation sheets to collect concrete data on the groups' functioning facilitate whole-class and small-group processing.

Class ends with another meeting of the base groups. Often members sign a contract as to how they will apply what they have learned. Longer class periods, three-hour sessions, for example, can be structured like a 90-minute class period with the addition of more than one formal cooperative learning activity during class time.

Cooperative Learning and the State of the Art

The Cooperative Learning Center at the University of Minnesota has consistently engaged in five interrelated activities: reviewing and synthesizing the research, developing theory, using systematic research programs to validate or disconfirm theory, operationalizing the research into the state-of-the-art use of cooperative learning, and engaging in long-term efforts to implement cooperative learning in a network of colleges and school districts throughout the United States, Canada, Europe, the Pacific Rim, the Middle East, and other parts of the world.

The state-of-the-art use of cooperative learning has changed substantially since the initial conceptualization of the theory by Morton Deutsch in 1949. Deutsch's initial theory had interdependence as the central feature. Positive interdependence is still the essential element of cooperative learning, but it has been refined as the understanding of how the different ways of structuring it interact with each other has increased (see Johnson and Johnson 1989a). The other four essential elements that mediate the effectiveness of cooperative learning are continually being redefined and calibrated, modifying how cooperative learning is best structured in classrooms. While the authors used formal, informal, and base groups in their college teaching in the 1960s, the definition of each and many of the specific operationalizations of cooperation within each type of cooperative group have been considerably redefined since then.

The changes that have occurred in the past 20 years—and are continuing to occur—reflect the dynamic nature of cooperative learning and that the state of the art of cooperation is advancing through a process of progressive refinement. The changes that have occurred in the development of cooperative learning represent a progressive refinement in the state of the art. Improvement is expected to continue, because cooperative learning is a dynamic activity in education, and the research investigating its nature and use continues.

Looking Forward

The end of this book is a new beginning. Years of experience in using cooperative learning in the classroom are needed to gain expertise in its use, and much more remains to learn. The addition of informal cooperative learning activities and long-term permanent base groups will increase the power and effectiveness of cooperation in the classroom. Teaching students more and more sophisticated social skills will improve how well they work together to maximize their learning. Supplementing the use of cooperative learning with appropriate competitions and individual assignments will further enrich the quality of learning within the classroom. Structuring academic controversies in cooperative learning groups will move students to higher levels of reasoning and thinking while providing a considerable increase in energy and fun. Teaching students how to negotiate their differences and mediate each other's conflicts will accelerate their skills in managing conflicts in cooperative learning groups. Finally, moving cooperation to the college level by organizing faculty into cooperative teams will create a congruent organizational structure within which both faculty and students will thrive.

REFERENCES

The Educational Resources Information Center (ERIC) Clearinghouse
on Higher Education abstracts and indexes the current literature on
higher education for inclusion in ERIC's data base and announce-
ment in ERIC's monthly bibliographic journal, *Resources in Education* (RIE). Most of these publications are available through the
ERIC Document Reproduction Service (EDRS). For publications cited
in this bibliography that are available from EDRS, ordering number
and price code are included. Readers who wish to order a publication should write to the ERIC Document Reproduction Service,
7420 Fullerton Rd., Suite 110, Springfield VA 22153-2852. (Phone
orders with VISA or MasterCard are taken at 800-443-ERIC or
703-440-1400.) When ordering, please specify the document (ED)
number. Documents are available as noted in microfiche (MF) and
paper copy (PC). If you have the price code ready when you call
EDRS, an exact price can be quoted. The last page of the latest issue
of *Resources in Education* also has the current cost, listed by code.

Abrahamson, S. 21 October 1987. "Harvard Medical School Tries a
Problem-Based Curriculum." *Chronicle of Higher Education:*
B1–B2.

American Society for Training and Development. 1988. *Workplace
Basics: The Skills Employers Want.* Washington, D.C.: U.S. Dept.
of Labor.

Anderson, T., and B. Armbruster. 1982. "Reader and Text Studying
Strategies." In *Reading Expository Material,* edited by W. Otto and
S. White. New York: Academic Press.

Armento, B. 1977. "Teacher Behaviors Related to Student Achievement on a Social Science Concept Test." *Journal of Teacher Education* 28: 46–52.

Aronson, Elliot, N. Blaney, C. Stephan, J. Sikes, and M. Snapp. 1978.
The Jigsaw Classroom. Beverly Hills, Cal.: Sage.

Association of American Colleges. 1985. "Integrity in the Curriculum:
A Report to the Academic Community." Project on Redefining the
Meaning and Purpose of Baccalaureate Degrees. Washington, D.C.:
Author. ED 251 059. 62 pp. MF–01; PC–03.

Astin, Alexander W. 1977. *Four Critical Years: Effects of College on
Beliefs, Attitudes, and Knowledge.* San Francisco: Jossey-Bass.

———. 1985. *Achieving Educational Excellence.* San Francisco:
Jossey-Bass.

Astin, H.S., A.W. Astin, A. Bisconti, and H. Frankel. 1972. *Higher Education and the Disadvantaged Student.* Washington, D.C.: Human
Science Press.

Atkinson, R.C., and R.M. Shiffrin. 1971. "The Control of Short-Term
Memory." *Scientific American* 225: 82–90.

Ausubel, David. 1963. *The Psychology of Meaningful Verbal Learning.*
New York: Grune & Straton.

Baldwin, Roger G. 1982. "Fostering Faculty Vitality: Options for Institutions and Administrators." Washington, D.C.: American Association of University Administrators. ED 220 069. 8 pp. MF–01; PC–01.

Barnes, Carol P. 1980. "Questions: The Untapped Resource." Paper presented at the annual meeting of the American Educational Research Association, Boston. ED 188 555. 42 pp. MF–01; PC–02.

———. 1983. "Questioning in the College Classroom." In *Studies in College Teaching,* edited by C.L. Ellner and C.P. Barnes. Lexington, Mass.: Lexington Books.

Blake, Robert, and Jane Mouton. 1974. "Designing Change for Educational Institutions through the D/D Matrix." *Education and Urban Society* 6: 179–204.

Blanc, R.A., L.E. Debuhr, and D.C. Martin. 1983. "Breaking the Attrition Cycle: The Effects of Supplemental Instruction on Undergraduate Performance and Attrition." *Journal of Higher Education* 54: 80–90.

Bligh, Donald A. 1972. *What's the Use of Lectures?* Harmondsworth, Eng.: Penguin.

Blumberg, A., J. May, and R. Perry. 1974. "An Inner-City School That Changed—and Continued to Change." *Education and Urban Society* 6: 222–38.

Bok, E.L. 1986. *Higher Learning.* Cambridge, Mass.: Harvard Univ. Press.

Bouton, Clark, and Russell Garth, eds. 1983. *Learning in Groups.* New Directions for Teaching and Learning No. 14. San Francisco: Jossey-Bass.

Bovard, E. 1951a. "The Experimental Production of Interpersonal Affect." *Journal of Abnormal Psychology* 46: 521–28.

———. 1951b. "Group Structure and Perception." *Journal of Abnormal and Social Psychology* 46: 398–405.

Bowen, Donald D., and Conrad N. Jackson. 1985–86. "Curing Those Ol' 'Omigod-Not-Another-Group-Class' Blues." *Organizational Behavior Teaching Review* 10(4): 21–31.

Bowers, J.W. 1986. "Classroom Communication Apprehension: A Survey." *Communication Education* 35(4): 372–78.

Boyer, Ernest L. 1987. *College: The Undergraduate Experience in America.* New York: Harper & Row.

———. 1991. *Scholarship Reconsidered: Priorities of the Professoriat.* Carnegie Foundation for the Advancement of Teaching. Lawrenceville, N.J.: Princeton Univ. Press. ED 326 149. 151 pp. MF–01; PC–07.

Broadbent, D.E. 1970. "Review Lecture." *Proclamations of the Royal Society* 1: 333–50.

Brown, John S., Allan Collins, and Paul Duguid. 1989. "Situated Cognition and the Culture of Learning." *Educational Researcher* 18(1): 32–42.

Bruner, Jerome. 1960. *The Process of Education.* Cambridge, Mass.: Harvard Univ. Press.

Burns, Marilyn. 1987. *A Collection of Math Lessons.* New Rochelle, N.Y.: Cuisenaire Co.

Campbell, J. 1965. "The Children's Crusader: Colonel Francis W. Parker." Ph.D. dissertation, Columbia Univ., Teachers College.

Cohen, Elizabeth. 1986. *Designing Groupwork.* New York: Columbia Univ., Teachers College Press.

Collins, B. 1970. *Social Psychology.* Reading, Mass.: Addison-Wesley.

Cooper, James. 1990. "Cooperative Learning and College Teaching: Tips from the Trenches." *Teaching Professor* 4(5): 1–2.

Costin, Frank. 1972. "Lecturing versus Other Methods of Teaching: A Review of Research." *British Journal of Educational Technology* 3(1): 4–30.

Dansereau, Donald. 1985. "Learning Strategy Research." In *Thinking and Learning Skills,* edited by J. Segal, S. Chipman, and R. Glaser. Hillsdale, N.J.: Erlbaum Associates.

———. 1987. "Transfer from Cooperative to Individual Studying." *Journal of Reading* 30: 614–18.

Deutsch, Morton. 1958. "Trust and Suspicion." *Journal of Conflict Resolution* 2: 25–279.

———. 1960. "The Effects of Motivational Orientation upon Trust and Suspicion." *Human Relations* 13: 123–39.

———. 1962. "Cooperation and Trust: Some Theoretical Notes." In *Nebraska Symposium on Motivation,* edited by M.R. Jones. Lincoln: Univ. of Nebraska Press.

Deutsch, Morton, and R. Krauss. 1962. "Studies of Interpersonal Bargaining." *Journal of Conflict Resolution* 6: 52–76.

DeVries, David, and Keith Edwards. 1973. "Learning Games and Student Teams: Their Effects on Classroom Process." *American Educational Research Journal* 10: 307–18.

———. 1974. "Student Teams and Learning Games: Their Effects on Cross-Race and Cross-Sex Interaction." *Journal of Educational Psychology* 66(5): 741–49.

Dewey, John. 1916. *Democracy and Education.* New York: Macmillan.

DiPardo, A., and S. Freedman. 1988. "Peer Response Groups in the Writing Classroom: Theoretic Foundations and New Directions." *Review of Educational Research* 58: 119–50.

Eble, K. 1983. *The Aims of College Teaching.* San Francisco: Jossey-Bass.

Eison, James. 1990. "Confidence in the College Classroom: Ten Maxims for New Teachers." *College Teaching* 38(1): 21–25.

Fosnot, Catherine T. 1989. *Enquiring Teachers, Enquiring Learners: A Constructivist Approach for Teaching.* New York: Columbia Univ., Teachers College Press.

Gabbert, Barbara, David W. Johnson, and Roger Johnson. 1986.

"Cooperative Learning, Group-to-Individual Transfer, Process Gain, and the Acquisition of Cognitive Reasoning Strategies." *Journal of Psychology* 120(3): 265–78.

Gabelnick, Faith, Jean MacGregor, Roberta Matthews, and Barbara Smith, eds. 1990. *Learning Communities: Creating Connections among Students, Faculty, and Disciplines.* New Directions for Teaching and Learning No. 41. San Francisco: Jossey-Bass.

Gagne, E. 1985. *The Cognitive Psychology of School Learning.* Boston: Little, Brown.

Gibbs, Jeanne. 1987. *Tribes: A Process for Social Development and Cooperative Learning.* Santa Rosa, Cal.: Center Source Publications.

Goldschmid, M.L. 1971. "The Learning Cell: An Instructional Innovation." *Learning and Development* 2: 1–6.

Good, T., and D. Grouws. 1977. "Teaching Effects: A Process-Product Study in Fourth Grade Mathematics Classrooms." *Journal of Teacher Education* 28: 49–54.

Guetzkow, H., E. Kelly, and W. McKeachie. 1954. "An Experimental Comparison of Recitation, Discussion, and Tutorial Methods in College Teaching." *Journal of Educational Psychology* 45: 193–209.

Harkins, S., and R. Petty. 1982. "The Effects of Task Difficulty and Task Uniqueness on Social Loafing." *Journal of Personality and Social Psychology* 43: 1214–29.

Hartley, J., and S. Marshall. 1974. "On Notes and Notetaking." *University Quarterly* 28: 225–35.

Hartup, Willard. 1976. "Peer Interaction and the Behavioral Development of the Individual Child." In *Psychology and Child Development,* edited by E. Schloper and R. Reicher. New York: Plenum Press.

Hill, G. 1982. "Group versus Individual Performance: Are $N + 1$ Heads Better Than One?" *Psychology Bulletin* 91: 517–39.

Hwong, N., A. Caswell, D.W. Johnson, and R. Johnson. 1990. "Effects of Cooperative and Individualistic Learning on Prospective Elementary Teachers' Music Achievement and Attitudes." Manuscript submitted for publication.

Ingham, A., G. Levinger, J. Graves, and V. Peckham. 1974. "The Ringelmann Effect: Studies of Group Size and Group Performance." *Journal of Personality and Social Psychology* 10: 371–84.

Johnson, David W. 1971. "Role Reversal: A Summary and Review of the Research." *International Journal of Group Tensions* 1: 318–34.

———. 1973. "Communication in Conflict Situations: A Critical Review of the Research." *International Journal of Group Tensions* 3: 46–47.

———. 1974. "Communication and the Inducement of Cooperative Behavior in Conflicts: A Critical Review." *Speech Monographs* 41: 64–78.

———. 1979. *Educational Psychology.* Englewood Cliffs, N.J.: Prentice-Hall.

———. 1980. "Constructive Peer Relationships, Social Development, and Cooperative Learning Experiences: Implications for the Prevention of Drug Abuse." *Journal of Drug Education* 10: 7–24.

———. 1990. *Reaching Out: Interpersonal Effectiveness and Self-Actualization.* 4th ed. Englewood Cliffs, N.J.: Prentice-Hall.

———. 1991. *Human Relations and Your Career.* 3d ed. Englewood Cliffs, N.J.: Prentice-Hall.

Johnson, David W., and Frank Johnson. 1991. *Joining Together: Group Theory and Group Skills.* 4th ed. Englewood Cliffs, N.J.: Prentice-Hall.

Johnson, David W., and Roger T. Johnson. 1974. "Instructional Goal Structure: Cooperative, Competitive, or Individualistic." *Review of Educational Research* 44: 213–40.

———. 1978. "Cooperative, Competitive, and Individualistic Learning." *Journal of Research and Development in Education* 12: 3–15.

———. 1979. "Conflict in the Classroom: Controversy and Learning." *Review of Educational Research* 49: 51–70.

———. 1981. "Effects of Cooperative and Individualistic Learning Experiences on Interethnic Interaction." *Journal of Educational Psychology* 73(3): 454–59.

———. 1983. "The Socialization and Achievement Crisis: Are Cooperative Learning Experiences the Solution?" In *Applied Social Psychology Annual 4,* edited by L. Bickman. Beverly Hills, Cal.: Sage.

———. 1987. *Creative Conflict.* Edina, Minn.: Interaction Book Co.

———. 1989a. *Cooperation and Competition: Theory and Research.* Edina, Minn.: Interaction Book Co.

———. 1989b. "Impact of Goal and Resource Interdependence on Problem-Solving Success." *Journal of Social Psychology* 129(5): 621–29.

———. 1989c. *Leading the Cooperative School.* Edina, Minn.: Interaction Book Co.

———. 1991. *Learning Together and Alone: Cooperative, Competitive, and Individualistic Learning.* Englewood Cliffs, N.J.: Prentice-Hall.

Johnson, David W., Roger Johnson, and Edythe Holubec. 1990. *Circles of Learning: Cooperation in the Classroom.* Edina, Minn.: Interaction Book Co.

———. 1991a. *Advanced Cooperative Learning.* Edina, Minn.: Interaction Book Co.

———. 1991b. *Cooperation in the Classroom.* Edina, Minn.: Interaction Book Co.

Johnson, David W., Roger Johnson, and Geoffrey Maruyama. 1983. "Interdependence and Interpersonal Attraction among Heterogeneous and Homogeneous Individuals: A Theoretical Formulation and a Meta-Analysis of the Research." *Review of Educational*

Research 53: 5–54.

Johnson, David W., Roger Johnson, Ann Ortiz, and Marybeth Stanne. *In press.* "Impact of Positive Goal and Resource Interdependence on Achievement, Interaction, and Attitudes." Manuscript submitted for publication.

Johnson, David W., Roger Johnson, and Karl Smith. 1986. "Academic Conflict among Students: Controversy and Learning." In *Social Psychological Applications to Education,* edited by R. Feldman. Cambridge: Cambridge Univ. Press.

Johnson, David W., Roger Johnson, Mary Stanne, and Antoine Garibaldi. 1990. "The Impact of Leader and Member Group Processing on Achievement in Cooperative Groups." *Journal of Social Psychology* 130: 507–16.

Johnson, David W., Geoffrey Maruyama, Roger Johnson, Deborah Nelson, and Linda Skon. 1981. "Effects of Cooperative, Competitive, and Individualistic Goal Structures on Achievement: A Meta-Analysis." *Psychology Bulletin* 89: 47–62.

Johnson, David W., and R. Matross. 1977. "The Interpersonal Influence of the Psychotherapist." In *The Effective Therapist: A Handbook,* edited by A. Gurman and A. Razin. Elmsford, N.Y.: Pergamon Press.

Johnson, David W., and Patricia Noonan. 1972. "Effects of Acceptance and Reciprocation of Self-Disclosures on the Development of Trust." *Journal of Counselling Psychology* 19(5): 411–16.

Johnson, David W., Linda Skon, and Roger Johnson. 1980. "Effects of Cooperative, Competitive, and Individualistic Conditions on Children's Problem-Solving Performance." *American Educational Research Journal* 17(1): 83–94.

Kagan, Spencer. 1988. *Cooperative Learning.* San Juan Capistrano, Cal.: Resources for Teachers.

Karp, D., and W. Yoels. 1987. "The College Classroom: Some Observations on the Meanings of Student Participation." *Sociology and Social Research* 60: 421–39.

Keppel, G., and B. Underwood. 1962. "Proactive Inhibition in Short-Term Retention of Single Items." *Journal of Verbal Learning and Verbal Behavior* 1: 153–61.

Kerr, N. 1983. "The Dispensability of Member Effort and Group Motivation Losses: Free-Rider Effects." *Journal of Personality and Social Psychology* 44: 78–94.

Kerr, N., and S. Bruun. 1983. "The Dispensability of Member Effort and Group Motivation Losses: Free-Rider Effects." *Journal of Personality and Social Psychology* 44: 78–94.

Kiewra, Kenneth. 1985a. "Investigating Notetaking and Review: A Depth of Processing Alternatives." *Educational Psychologist* 20(1): 23–32.

———. 1985b. "Providing the Instructor's Notes: An Effective Addition to Student Learning." *Educational Psychologist* 20(1):

33–39.

———. 1987. "Notetaking and Review: The Research and Its Implications." *Instructional Science* 16: 233–49.

Kiewra, K., and S. Benton. 1988. "The Relationship between Information-Processing Ability and Notetaking." *Contemporary Educational Psychology* 13: 33–44.

Kouzes, J., and B. Posner. 1987. *The Leadership Challenge.* San Francisco: Jossey-Bass.

Kulik, J.A., and C.L.L. Kulik. 1979. "College Teaching." In *Research on Teaching: Concepts, Findings, and Implications,* edited by P.L. Peterson and H.J. Walberg. Berkeley, Cal.: McCutcheon.

Lamm, H., and G. Trommsdorff. 1973. "Group versus Individual Performance on Tasks Requiring Ideational Proficiency (Brainstorming): A Review." *European Journal of Social Psychology* 3: 361–88.

Langer, E., and A. Benevento. 1978. "Self-Induced Dependence." *Journal of Personality and Social Psychology* 36: 886–93.

Latane, B., K. Williams, and S. Harkins. 1979. "Many Hands Make Light the Work: The Causes and Consequences of Social Loafing." *Journal of Personality and Social Psychology* 37: 822–32.

Lave, J. 1988. *Cognition in Practice: Mind, Mathematics, and Culture in Everyday Life.* Cambridge: Cambridge Univ. Press.

Levin, H., G. Glass, and G. Meister. 1984. *Cost-Effectiveness of Educational Interventions.* Stanford, Cal.: Institute for Research on Educational Finance and Governance.

Lew, Marvin, Debra Mesch, David W. Johnson, and Roger Johnson. 1986a. "Components of Cooperative Learning: Effects of Collaborative Skills and Academic Group Contingencies on Achievement and Mainstreaming." *Contemporary Educational Psychology* 11: 229–39.

———. 1986b. "Positive Interdependence, Academic and Collaborative-Skills Group Contingencies, and Isolated Students." *American Educational Research Journal* 23: 476–88.

Light, Richard J. 1990. *The Harvard Assessment Seminars.* Cambridge, Mass.: Harvard Univ.

Little, J. 1981. "School Success and Staff Development in Urban Desegregated Schools." Paper presented at a meeting of the American Educational Research Association, April, Los Angeles, California.

MacGregor, Jean. 1990. "Collaborative Learning: Shared Inquiry as a Process of Reform." In *The Changing Face of College Teaching,* edited by Marilla Svinicki. New Directions for Teaching and Learning No. 42. San Francisco: Jossey-Bass.

McKeachie, Wilbert. 1951. "Anxiety in the College Classroom." *Journal of Educational Research* 45: 153–60.

———. 1954. "Individual Conformity to Attitudes of Classroom Groups." *Journal of Abnormal and Social Psychology* 49: 282–89.

———. 1967. "Research in Teaching: The Gap between Theory and

Practice." In *Improving College Teaching*, edited by C. Lee. Washington, D.C.: American Council on Education.

————. 1986. *Teaching Tips: A Guidebook for the Beginning College Teacher*. 8th ed. Boston: D.C. Heath.

————. September 1988. "Teaching Thinking." *Update* 2(1): 1.

McKeachie, Wilbert, and J. Kulik. 1975. "Effective College Training." In *Review of Research in Education*, edited by F. Kerlinger. Itasca, Ill.: Peacock.

McKeachie, Wilbert, Paul Pintrich, Lin Yi-Guang, and David Smith. 1986. *Teaching and Learning in the College Classroom: A Review of the Research Literature*. Ann Arbor: Regents of the Univ. of Michigan.

Mackworth, J. 1970. *Vigilance and Habituation*. Harmondsworth, Eng.: Penguin.

May, M., and L. Doob. 1937. "Competition and Cooperation." *Social Science Research Council Bulletin* No. 25. New York: Social Science Research Council.

Menges, Robert. 1988. "Research on Teaching and Learning: The Relevant and the Redundant." *Review of Higher Education* 11(3): 259-68.

Mesch, Debra, David W. Johnson, and Roger Johnson. 1988. "Impact of Positive Interdependence and Academic Group Contingencies on Achievement." *Journal of Social Psychology* 128: 345-52.

Mesch, D., M. Lew, D.W. Johnson, and R. Johnson. 1986. "Isolated Teenagers, Cooperative Learning, and the Training of Social Skills." *Journal of Psychology* 120: 323-34.

Moede, W. 1927. "Die Richtlinien der Leistungs-psychologie." *Industrielle Psychotechnik* 4: 193-207.

Motley, M.T. January 1988. "Taking the Terror out of Talk." *Psychology Today* 22(1): 46-49.

Murray, F. 1983. "Cognitive Benefits of Teaching on the Teacher." Paper presented at an annual meeting of the American Educational Research Association, Montreal, Quebec.

Murray, H.G. 1985. "Classroom Teaching Behaviors Related to College Teaching Effectiveness." In *Using Research to Improve Teaching*, edited by J.G. Donald and A.M. Sullivan. San Francisco: Jossey-Bass.

National Center for Education Statistics. 1984. *Two Years after High School: A Capsule Description of 1980 Seniors*. Washington, D.C.: U.S. Dept. of Education. ED 250 464. 84 pp. MF-01; PC-04.

National Institute of Education. 1984. *Involvement in Learning*. Study Group on the Conditions of Excellence in Higher Education. Washington, D.C.: Author. ED 246 833. 127 pp. MF-01; PC-06.

Neer, M.R. 1987. "The Development of an Instrument to Measure Classroom Apprehension." *Communication Education* 36: 154-66.

Noel, L. 1985. "Increasing Student Retention: New Challenges and

Potential." In *Increasing Student Retention: Effective Programs and Practices for Reducing the Dropout Rate,* edited by L. Noel, R.F. Levitz, and D. Saluri. San Francisco: Jossey-Bass.

Pascarella, E.T. 1980. "Student-Faculty Informal Contact and College Outcomes." *Review of Educational Research* 50: 545–95.

Pelz, Donald, and Frank Andrews. 1976. *Scientists in Organizations: Productive Climates for Research and Development.* Ann Arbor: Univ. of Michigan, Institute for Social Research.

Penner, Jon. 1984. *Why Many College Teachers Cannot Lecture.* Springfield, Ill.: Charles C. Thomas.

Pepitone, Emmy. 1980. *Children in Cooperation and Competition.* Lexington, Mass.: Lexington Books.

Petty, R., S. Harkins, K. Williams, and B. Latane. 1977. "The Effects of Group Size on Cognitive Effort and Evaluation." *Personality and Social Psychology Bulletin* 3: 575–78.

Romer, Karen, ed. 1985. *CUE: Models of Collaboration in Undergraduate Education.* Providence, R.I.: Brown Univ. Press.

Rosenshine, Barak. December 1968. "To Explain: A Review of Research." *Educational Leadership* 26: 303–9.

Rosenshine, Barak, and R. Stevens. 1986. "Teaching Functions." In *Handbook of Research on Teaching,* edited by M.C. Wittrock. 3d ed. New York: Macmillan.

Ruggiero, V.R. 1988. *Teaching Thinking across the Curriculum.* New York: Harper & Row.

Ruhl, K., C. Hughes, and P. Schloss. 1987. "Using the Pause Procedure to Enhance Lecture Recall." *Teacher Education and Special Education* 10(1): 14–18.

Salomon, G. 1981. "Communication and Education: Social and Psychological Interactions." *People and Communication* 13: 9–271.

Schoenfeld, A.H. 1985. *Mathematical Problem Solving.* Orlando: Academic Press.

———. 1989. "Ideas in the Air: Speculations on Small-Group Learning, Peer Interactions, Cognitive Apprenticeship, Quasi-Vygotskean Notions of Internalization, Creativity, Problem Solving, and Mathematical Practice." *International Journal of Education Research.*

Scully, M.G. October 1981. "One Million Students at U.S. Colleges; Triple Present Number Seems Likely by 1990." *Chronicle of Higher Education:* 1.

Sharan, Shlomo. 1980. "Cooperative Learning in Teams: Recent Methods and Effects on Achievement, Attitudes, and Ethnic Relations." *Review of Educational Research* 50: 241–72.

Sharan, Shlomo, and Yael Sharan. 1976. *Small-Group Teaching.* Englewood Cliffs, N.J.: Educational Technology Publications.

Sheahan, Bonney H., and John A. White. 1990. "Quo Vadis, Undergraduate Engineering Education?" *Engineering Education* 80(8): 1017–22.

Sheingold, K., J. Hawkins, and C. Char. 1984. "I'm the Thinkist, You're the Typist: The Interaction of Technology and the Social Life of Classrooms." *Journal of Social Issues* 40(3): 49–56.

Skon, L., D.W. Johnson, and R. Johnson. 1981. "Cooperative Peer Interaction versus Individual Competition and Individualistic Efforts: Effects on the Acquisition of Cognitive Reasoning Strategies." *Journal of Educational Psychology* 73(1): 83–92.

Slavin, Robert E. 1980. "Cooperative Learning." *Review of Educational Research* 50: 315–42.

———. 1983. *Cooperative Learning.* New York: Longman.

———. 1990. *Cooperative Learning: Theory, Research, and Practice.* Englewood Cliffs, N.J.: Prentice-Hall.

Slavin, Robert, Marshall Leavey, and Nancy Madden. 1982. *Team-assisted Individualization: Mathematics Teacher's Manual.* Baltimore: Johns Hopkins Univ., Center for Social Organization of Schools.

Smith, D.G. 1980. "Instruction and Outcomes in an Undergraduate Setting." Paper presented at an annual meeting of the American Educational Research Association, Boston.

Smith, Karl A. 1986. "Cooperative Learning Groups." In *Strategies for Active Teaching and Learning in University Classrooms,* edited by Stephen F. Schomberg. Minneapolis: Univ. of Minnesota.

Smith, L., and M. Land. 1981. "Low-inference Verbal Behaviors Related to Teaching Clarity." *Journal of Classroom Interaction* 17: 37–42.

Starfield, Anthony M., Karl A. Smith, and Andrew L. Bleloch. 1990. *How to Model It: Problem Solving for the Computer Age.* New York: McGraw-Hill.

Stones, E. 1970. "Students' Attitudes to the Size of Teaching Groups." *Educational Review* 21(2): 98–108.

Stuart, John, and R. Rutherford. September 1978. "Medical Student Concentration during Lectures." *Lancet* 2: 514–16.

Terenzini, P.T. 1986. "Retention Research: Academic and Social Fit." Paper presented at a meeting of the Southern Regional Office of the College Entrance Examination Board, New Orleans.

Tinto, V. 1975. "Dropout from Higher Education: A Theoretical Synthesis of Recent Research." *Review of Educational Research* 45(1): 89–125.

———. 1987. *Leaving College: Rethinking the Causes and Cures of Student Attrition.* Chicago: Univ. of Chicago Press.

Treisman, P.U. 1985. "A Study of the Mathematics Performance of Black Students at the University of California, Berkeley." Ph.D. dissertation, Univ. of California–Berkeley.

Verner, Coolie, and Gary Dickinson. 1967. "The Lecture: An Analysis and Review of Research." *Adult Education* 17: 85–100.

Vygotsky, L. 1978. *Mind and Society.* Cambridge, Mass.: Harvard Univ. Press.

Wales, C., and R. Stager. 1978. *The Guided-Design Approach.* Englewood Cliffs, N.J.: Educational Technology Publications.

Watson, Goodwin, and David W. Johnson. 1972. *Social Psychology: Issues and Insights.* Philadelphia: Lippincott.

Waugh, N.C., and D.A. Norman. 1965. "Primary Memory." *Psychological Review* 72: 89–104.

Webb, N., P. Ender, and S. Lewis. 1986. "Problem-solving Strategies and Group Processes in Small Groups Learning Computer Programming." *American Educational Research Journal* 23(2): 243–61.

White, R., and R. Tisher. 1986. "Research on Natural Sciences." In *Handbook of Research on Teaching,* edited by M. Whittrock. 3d ed. New York: Macmillan.

Whitman, Neal A. 1988. *Peer Teaching: To Teach Is to Learn Twice.* ASHE-ERIC Higher Education Report No. 4. Washington, D.C.: Association for the Study of Higher Education. ED 305 016. 103 pp. MF–01; PC–05.

Williams, K. 1981. "The Effects of Group Cohesiveness on Social Loafing." Paper presented at an annual meeting of the Midwestern Psychological Association, Detroit.

Williams, K., S. Harkins, and B. Latane. 1981. "Identifiability as a Deterrent to Social Loafing: Two Cheering Experiments." *Journal of Personality and Social Psychology* 40: 303–11.

Wilson, R.C. 1987. "Toward Excellence in Teaching." In *Techniques for Evaluating and Improving Instruction,* edited by L.M. Aleamoni. San Francisco: Jossey-Bass.

Wulff, D.H., J.D. Nyquist, and R.D. Abbott. 1987. "Students' Perception of Large Classes." In *Teaching Large Classes Well,* edited by M.E. Weimer. San Francisco: Jossey-Bass.

Yager, Stuart, David Johnson, and Roger Johnson. 1985. "Oral Discussion, Group-to-Individual Transfer, and Achievement in Cooperative Learning Groups." *Journal of Educational Psychology* 77(1): 60–66.

INDEX

Quincy Massachusetts public schools, 5
Quintilien, 4

R

Read-and-explain pairs, 98
Reciprocal observations, 118
Relationships
        long-term, 110
Restructuring of information, 9
Reward interdependence, 58
Runners, 72

S

Science experiments, 58
Self-esteem, 52
Self-induced helplessness, 15
Self-perception, 50
Small-group
        processing, 24
        skills, 21
Social
        development, 48
        intervention skills, 68
        involvements, 47
        loafing, 15
        perspective, 52
        skills, 20
        skills and objectives, 60
        support, 44, 46
Social interdependence, 38, 39, 44, 45, 53
        characteristics, 29
        research, 27
Student
        academic work attitudes, 111
        aggression, 49
        autonomy, 49
        egocentrism, 49
        empowerment, 9
        learning evaluation, 69
        loneliness, 49
        retention, 46
Students
        non-task-oriented, 61
        task-oriented, 61
Student-student interaction, 2
Subject areas, 42
Summarizers, 63

ASHE-ERIC HIGHER EDUCATION REPORTS

Since 1983, the Association for the Study of Higher Education (ASHE) and the Educational Resources Information Center (ERIC) Clearinghouse on Higher Education, a sponsored project of the School of Education and Human Development at The George Washington University, have cosponsored the *ASHE-ERIC Higher Education Report* series. The 1991 series is the twentieth overall and the third to be published by the School of Education and Human Development at the George Washington University.

Each monograph is the definitive analysis of a tough higher education problem, based on thorough research of pertinent literature and institutional experiences. Topics are identified by a national survey. Noted practitioners and scholars are then commissioned to write the reports, with experts providing critical reviews of each manuscript before publication.

Eight monographs (10 before 1985) in the ASHE-ERIC Higher Education Report series are published each year and are available on individual and subscription bases. Subscription to eight issues is $90.00 annually; $70 to members of AAHE, AIR, or AERA; and $60 to ASHE members. All foreign subscribers must include an additional $10 per series year for postage.

To order single copies of existing reports, use the order form on the last page of this book. Regular prices, and special rates available to members of AAHE, AIR, AERA and ASHE, are as follows:

Series	Regular	Members
1990 and 91	$17.00	$12.75
1988 and 89	15.00	11.25
1985 and 87	10.00	7.50
1983 and 84	7.50	6.00
before 1983	6.50	5.00

Price includes book rate postage within the U.S. For foreign orders, please add $1.00 per book. Fast United Parcel Service available within the contiguous U.S. at $2.50 for each order under $50.00, and calculated at 5% of invoice total for orders $50.00 or above.

All orders under $45.00 must be prepaid. Make check payable to ASHE-ERIC. For Visa or MasterCard, include card number, expiration date and signature. A bulk discount of 10% is available on orders of 15 or more books (not applicable on subscriptions).

Address order to
ASHE-ERIC Higher Education Reports
The George Washington University
1 Dupont Circle, Suite 630
Washington, DC 20036
Or phone (202) 296-2597
Write or call for a complete catalog of ASHE-ERIC Higher Education Reports.

1991 ASHE-ERIC Higher Education Reports

1. Active Learning: Creating Excitement in the Classroom
   Charles C. Bonwell and James A. Eison

2. Realizing Gender Equality in Higher Education: The Need to
   Integrate Work/Family Issues
   Nancy Hensel

3 Academic Advising for Student Success: A System of Shared
   Responsibility
   by Susan H. Frost

1990 ASHE-ERIC Higher Education Reports

1. The Campus Green: Fund Raising in Higher Education
   Barbara E. Brittingham and Thomas R. Pezzullo

2. The Emeritus Professor: Old Rank - New Meaning
   James E. Mauch, Jack W. Birch, and Jack Matthews

3. "High Risk" Students in Higher Education: Future Trends
   Dionne J. Jones and Betty Collier Watson

4. Budgeting for Higher Education at the State Level: Enigma,
   Paradox, and Ritual
   Daniel T. Layzell and Jan W. Lyddon

5. Proprietary Schools: Programs, Policies, and Prospects
   John B. Lee and Jamie P. Merisotis

6. College Choice: Understanding Student Enrollment Behavior
   Michael B. Paulsen

7. Pursuing Diversity: Recruiting College Minority Students
   Barbara Astone and Elsa Nuñez-Wormack

8. Social Consciousness and Career Awareness: Emerging Link
   in Higher Education
   John S. Swift, Jr.

1989 ASHE-ERIC Higher Education Reports

1. Making Sense of Administrative Leadership: The 'L' Word in
   Higher Education
   Estela M. Bensimon, Anna Neumann, and Robert Birnbaum

2. Affirmative Rhetoric, Negative Action: African-American and
   Hispanic Faculty at Predominantly White Universities
   Valora Washington and William Harvey

3. Postsecondary Developmental Programs: A Traditional Agenda
   with New Imperatives
   Louise M. Tomlinson

4. The Old College Try: Balancing Athletics and Academics in
   Higher Education
   John R. Thelin and Lawrence L. Wiseman

5. The Challenge of Diversity: Involvement or Alienation in the Academy?
   Daryl G. Smith

6. Student Goals for College and Courses: A Missing Link in Assessing and Improving Academic Achievement
   Joan S. Stark, Kathleen M. Shaw, and Malcolm A. Lowther

7. The Student as Commuter: Developing a Comprehensive Institutional Response
   Barbara Jacoby

8. Renewing Civic Capacity: Preparing College Students for Service and Citizenship
   Suzanne W. Morse

1988 ASHE-ERIC Higher Education Reports

1. The Invisible Tapestry: Culture in American Colleges and Universities
   George D. Kuh and Elizabeth J. Whitt

2. Critical Thinking: Theory, Research, Practice, and Possibilities
   Joanne Gainen Kurfiss

3. Developing Academic Programs: The Climate for Innovation
   Daniel T. Seymour

4. Peer Teaching: To Teach is To Learn Twice
   Neal A. Whitman

5. Higher Education and State Governments: Renewed Partnership, Cooperation, or Competition?
   Edward R. Hines

6. Entrepreneurship and Higher Education: Lessons for Colleges, Universities, and Industry
   James S. Fairweather

7. Planning for Microcomputers in Higher Education: Strategies for the Next Generation
   Reynolds Ferrante, John Hayman, Mary Susan Carlson, and Harry Phillips

8. The Challenge for Research in Higher Education: Harmonizing Excellence and Utility
   Alan W. Lindsay and Ruth T. Neumann

1987 ASHE-ERIC Higher Education Reports

1. Incentive Early Retirement Programs for Faculty: Innovative Responses to a Changing Environment
   Jay L. Chronister and Thomas R. Kepple, Jr.

1985 ASHE-ERIC Higher Education Reports

1. Flexibility in Academic Staffing: Effective Policies and Practices
   Kenneth P. Mortimer, Marque Bagshaw, and Andrew T. Masland

2. Associations in Action: The Washington, D.C. Higher Education Community
   Harland G. Bloland

3. And on the Seventh Day: Faculty Consulting and Supplemental Income
   Carol M. Boyer and Darrell R. Lewis

4. Faculty Research Performance: Lessons from the Sciences and Social Sciences
   John W. Creswell

5. Academic Program Review: Institutional Approaches, Expectations, and Controversies
   Clifton F. Conrad and Richard F. Wilson

6. Students in Urban Settings: Achieving the Baccalaureate Degree
   Richard C. Richardson, Jr. and Louis W. Bender

7. Serving More Than Students: A Critical Need for College Student Personnel Services
   Peter H. Garland

8. Faculty Participation in Decision Making: Necessity or Luxury?
   Carol E. Floyd

1984 ASHE-ERIC Higher Education Reports

1. Adult Learning: State Policies and Institutional Practices
   K. Patricia Cross and Anne-Marie McCartan

2. Student Stress: Effects and Solutions
   Neal A. Whitman, David C. Spendlove, and Claire H. Clark

3. Part-time Faulty: Higher Education at a Crossroads
   Judith M. Gappa

4. Sex Discrimination Law in Higher Education: The Lessons of the Past Decade. ED 252 169.*
   J. Ralph Lindgren, Patti T. Ota, Perry A. Zirkel, and Nan Van Gieson

5. Faculty Freedoms and Institutional Accountability: Interactions and Conflicts
   Steven G. Olswang and Barbara A. Lee

6. The High Technology Connection: Academic/Industrial Cooperation for Economic Growth
   Lynn G. Johnson

7. Employee Educational Programs: Implications for Industry and Higher Education. ED 258 501.*
   Suzanne W. Morse

8. Academic Libraries: The Changing Knowledge Centers of Colleges and Universities
   Barbara B. Moran

9. Futures Research and the Strategic Planning Process: Implications for Higher Education
   James L. Morrison, William L. Renfro, and Wayne I. Boucher

10. Faculty Workload: Research, Theory, and Interpretation
    Harold E. Yuker

1983 ASHE-ERIC Higher Education Reports

1. The Path to Excellence: Quality Assurance in Higher Education
   Laurence R. Marcus, Anita O. Leone, and Edward D. Goldberg

2. Faculty Recruitment, Retention, and Fair Employment: Obligations and Opportunities
   John S. Waggaman

3. Meeting the Challenges: Developing Faculty Careers. ED 232 516.*
   Michael C.T. Brooks and Katherine L. German

4. Raising Academic Standards: A Guide to Learning Improvement
   Ruth Talbott Keimig

5. Serving Learners at a Distance: A Guide to Program Practices
   Charles E. Feasley

6. Competence, Admissions, and Articulation: Returning to the Basics in Higher Education
   Jean L. Preer

7. Public Service in Higher Education: Practices and Priorities
   Patricia H. Crosson

8. Academic Employment and Retrenchment: Judicial Review and Administrative Action
   Robert M. Hendrickson and Barbara A. Lee

9. Burnout: The New Academic Disease. ED 242 255.*
   Winifred Albizu Meléndez and Rafael M. de Guzmán

10. Academic Workplace: New Demands, Heightened Tensions
    Ann E. Austin and Zelda F. Gamson

*Out-of-print. Available through EDRS. Call 1-800-443-ERIC.

ORDER FORM

Quantity   **Amount**

_____ Please begin my subscription to the 1991 *ASHE-ERIC Higher Education Reports* at $90.00, 33% off the cover price, starting with Report 1, 1991. _____

_____ Please send a complete set of the 1990 *ASHE-ERIC Higher Education Reports* at $80.00, 41% off the cover price. _____

_____ Outside the U.S., add $10.00 per series for postage. _____

Individual reports are avilable at the following prices:

1990 and 1991, $17.00	1983 and 1984, $7.50
1988 and 1989, $15.00	1982 and back, $6.50
1985 to 1987, $10.00	

Book rate postage within the U.S. is included. Outside U.S., please add $1.00 per book for postage. Fast U.P.S. shipping is available within the contiguous U.S. at $2.50 for each order under $50.00, and calculated at 5% of invoice total for orders $50.00 or above. All orders under $45.00 must be prepaid.

PLEASE SEND ME THE FOLLOWING REPORTS:

Quantity	Report No.	Year	Title	Amount

Subtotal:	
Foreign or UPS:	
Total Due:	

Please check one of the following:
- ☐ Check enclosed, payable to GWU-ERIC.
- ☐ Purchase order attached ($45.00 minimum).
- ☐ Charge my credit card indicated below:
  - ☐ Visa   ☐ MasterCard

Expiration Date _____

Name _____

Title _____

Institution _____

Address _____

City _____ State _____ Zip _____

Phone _____

Signature _____ Date _____

SEND ALL ORDERS TO:
ASHE-ERIC Higher Education Reports
The George Washington University
One Dupont Circle, Suite 630
Washington, DC 20036-1183
Phone: (202) 296-2597

Johnson, David W., 1940-

Cooperative learning :
increasing college
1991.